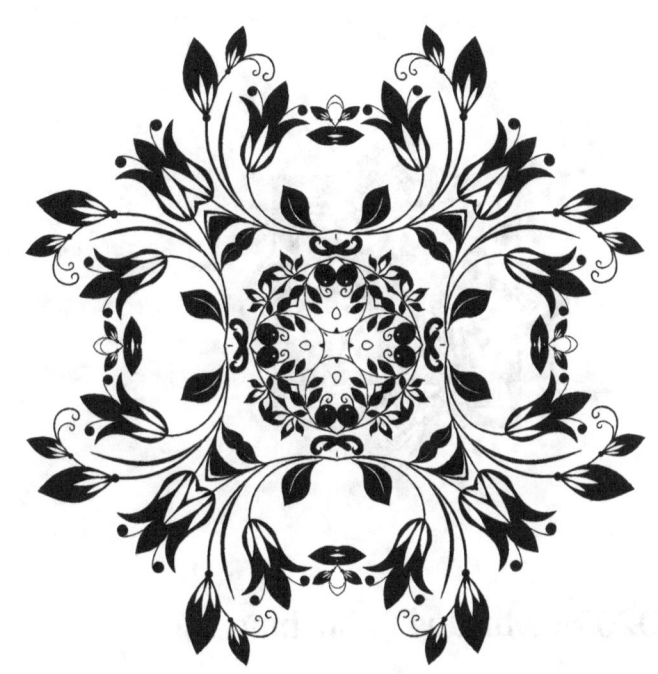

MANDALA

RELAXATION AND STRESS RELIEF

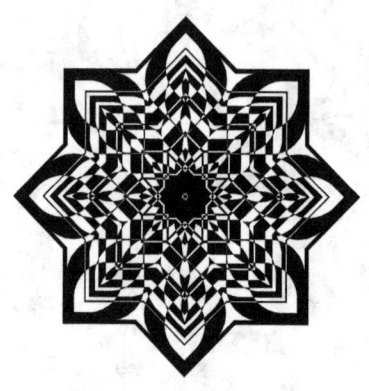

Copyright 2020 Newbridge Publishing

All Right Reserved

No part of this publication may be reproduced, distributed, or transmitted in any form or by any means, including photocopying, recording, or other electronic or mechanical methods, without the prior written permission of the Author, except in the case of brief quotations in critical reviews and certain other non commercial uses permitted by copyright law. For Permission requests, write to the Publisher.

Published by Newbridge Publishing

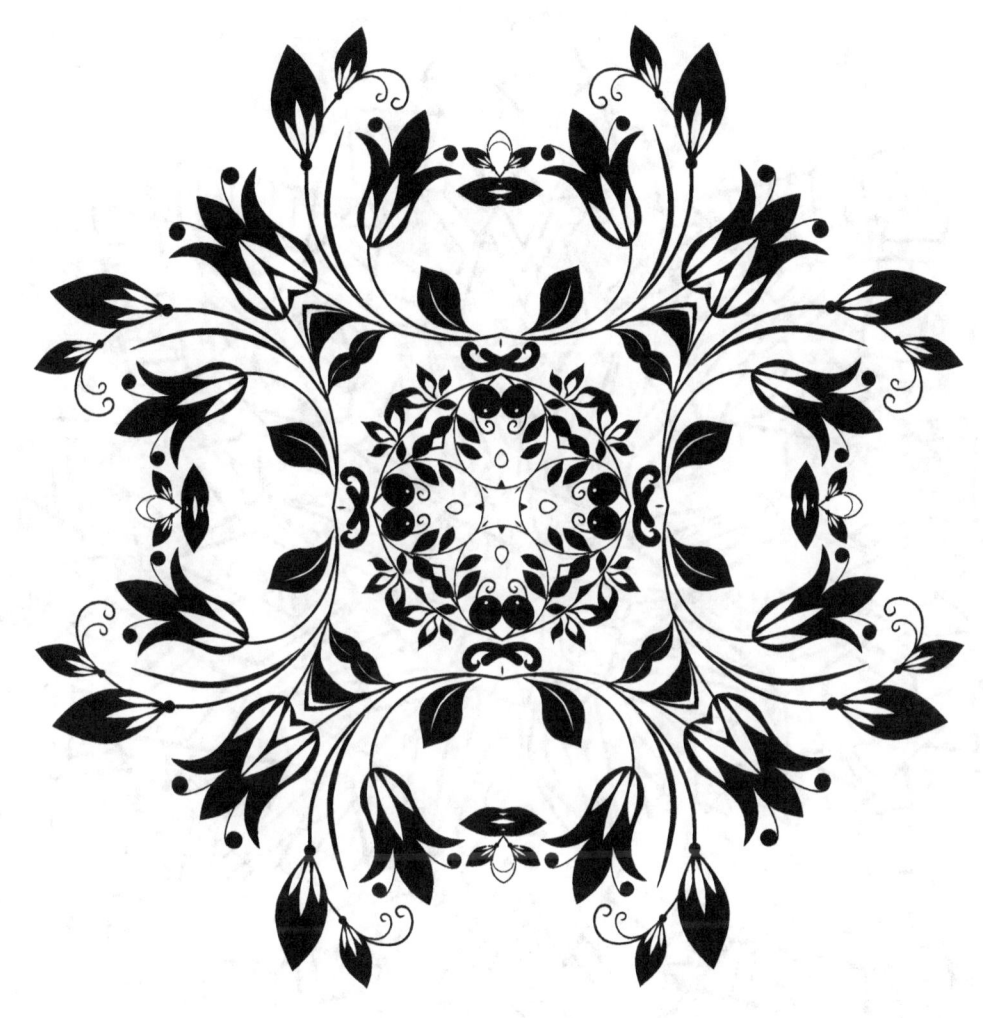

MANDALA COLOURING BOOK FOR ADULTS

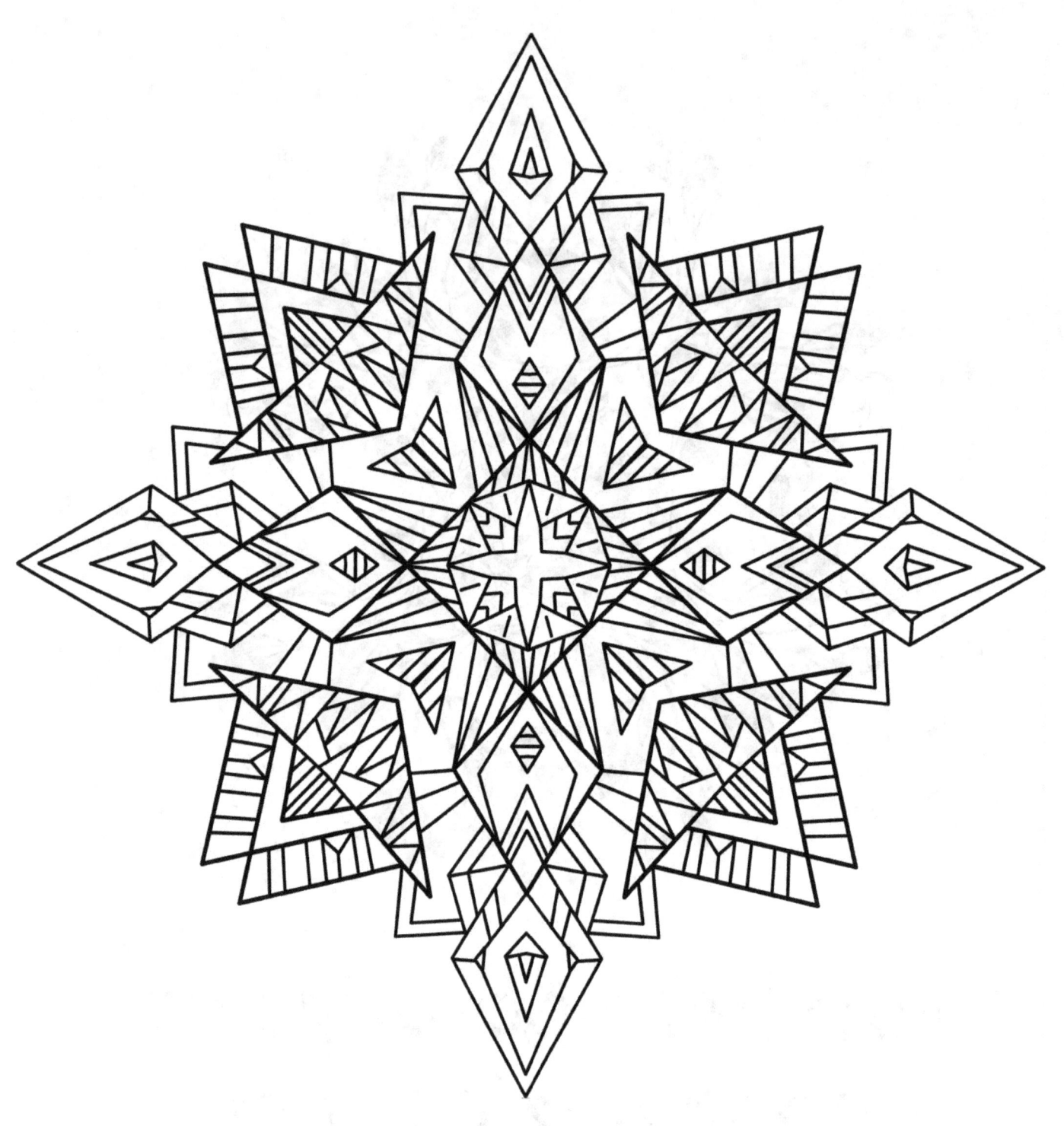

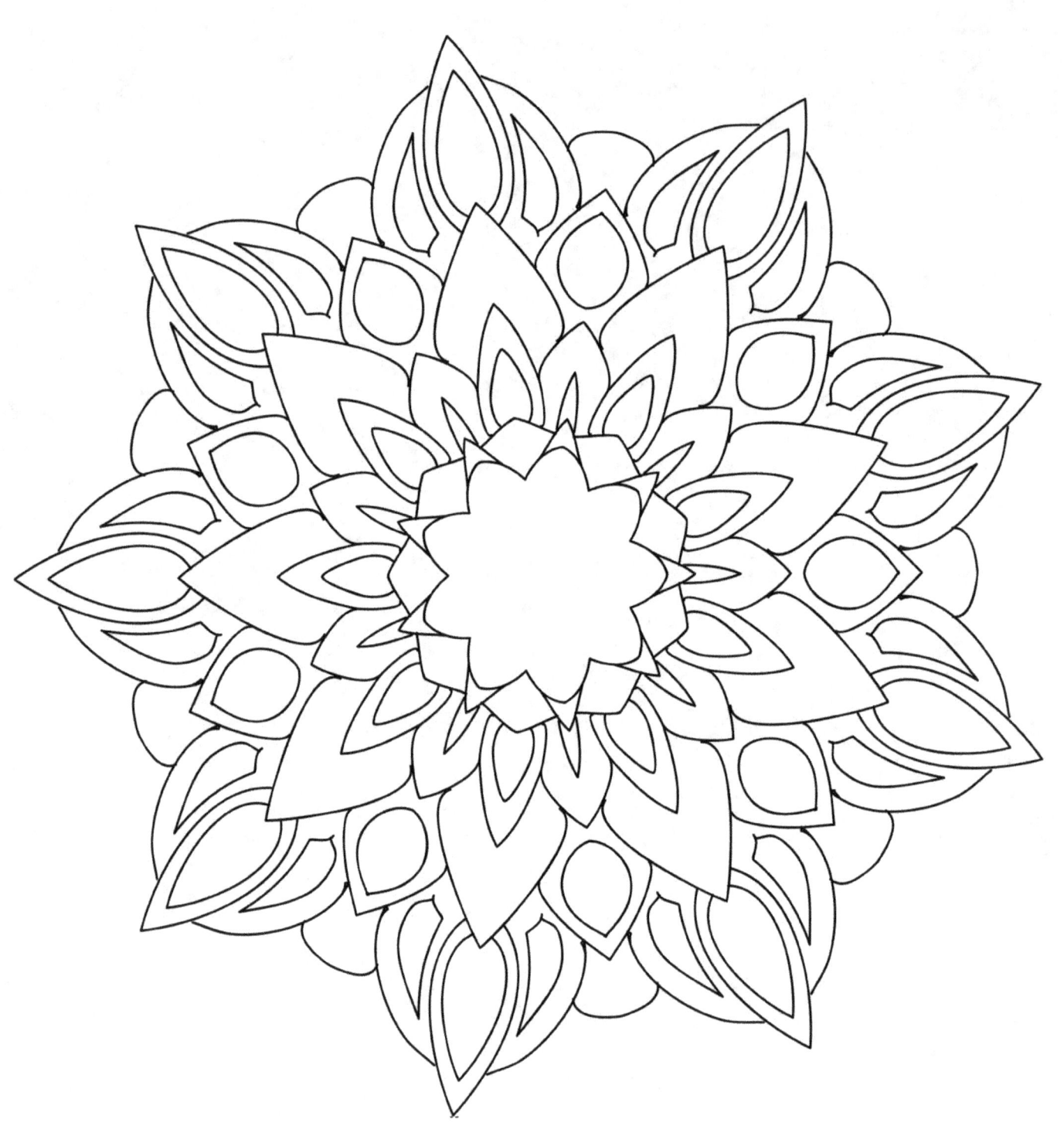

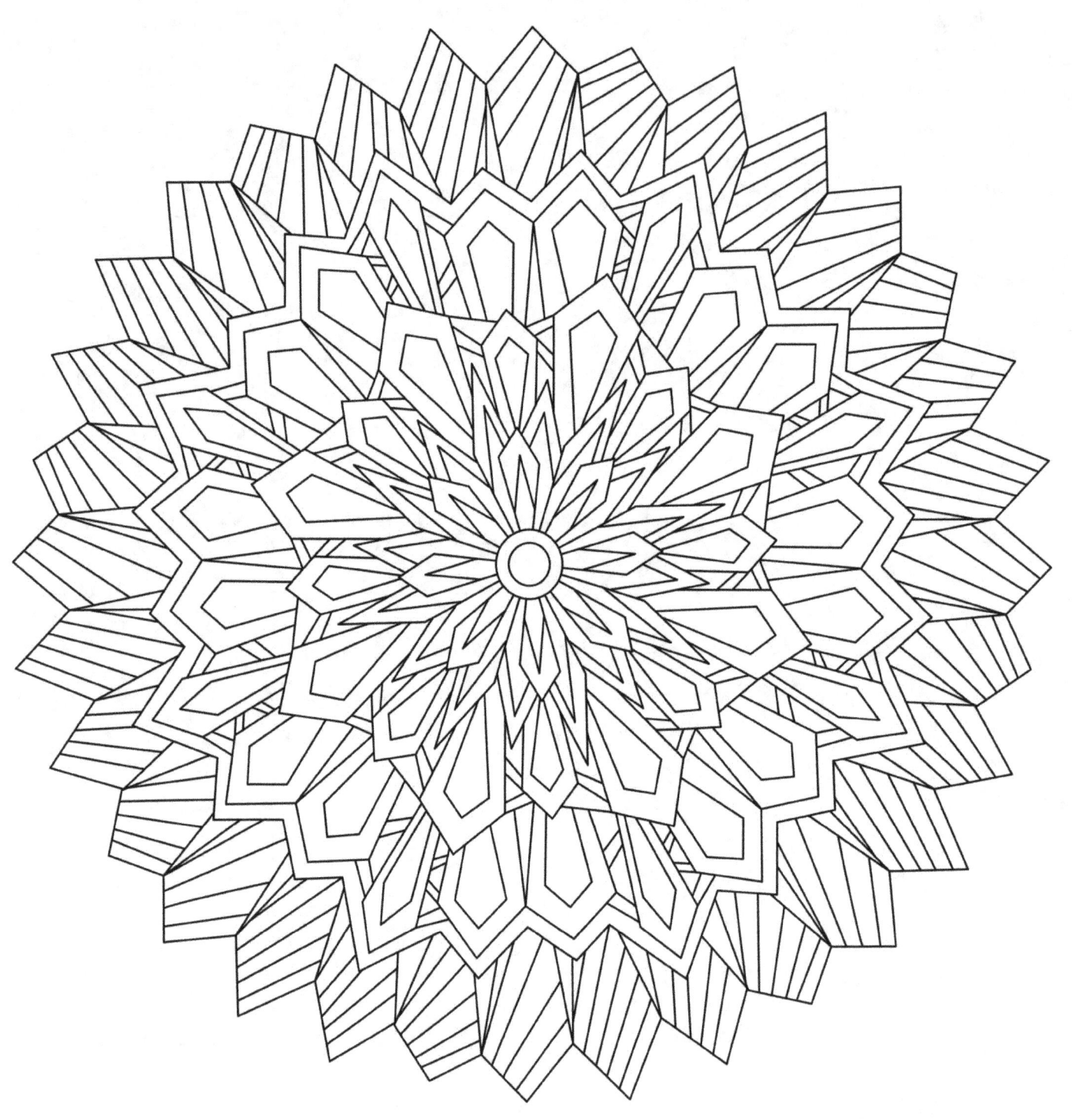

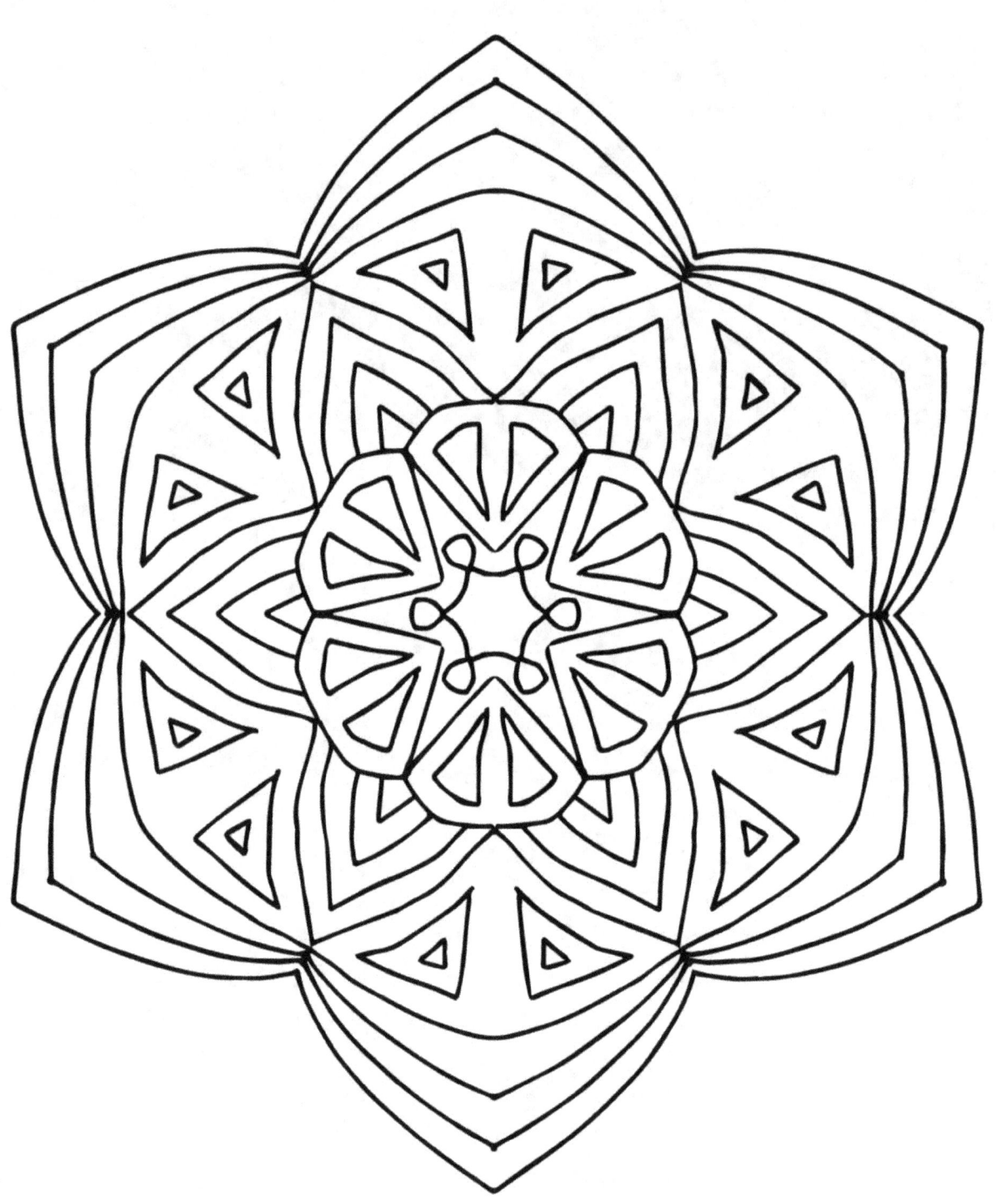

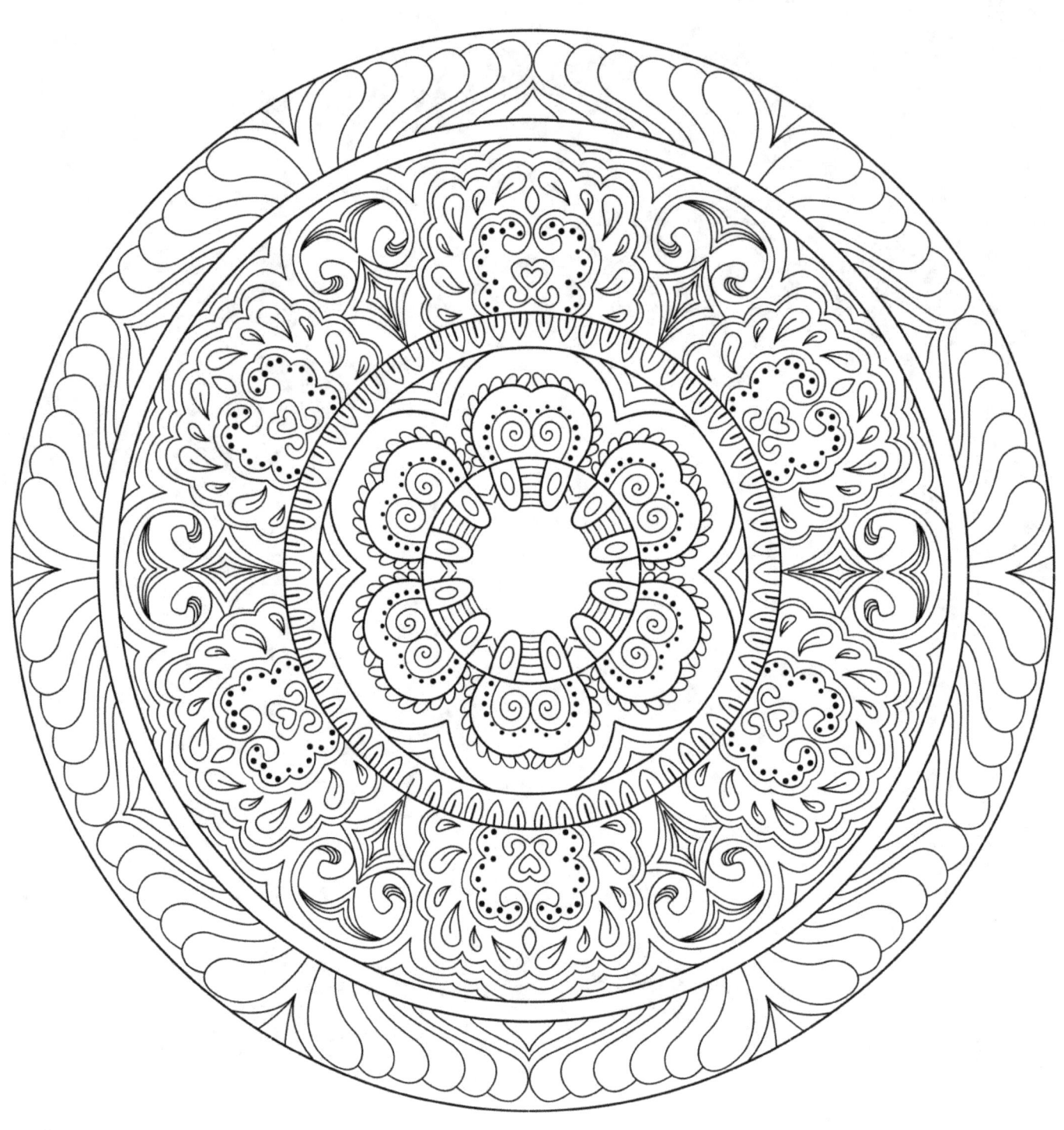

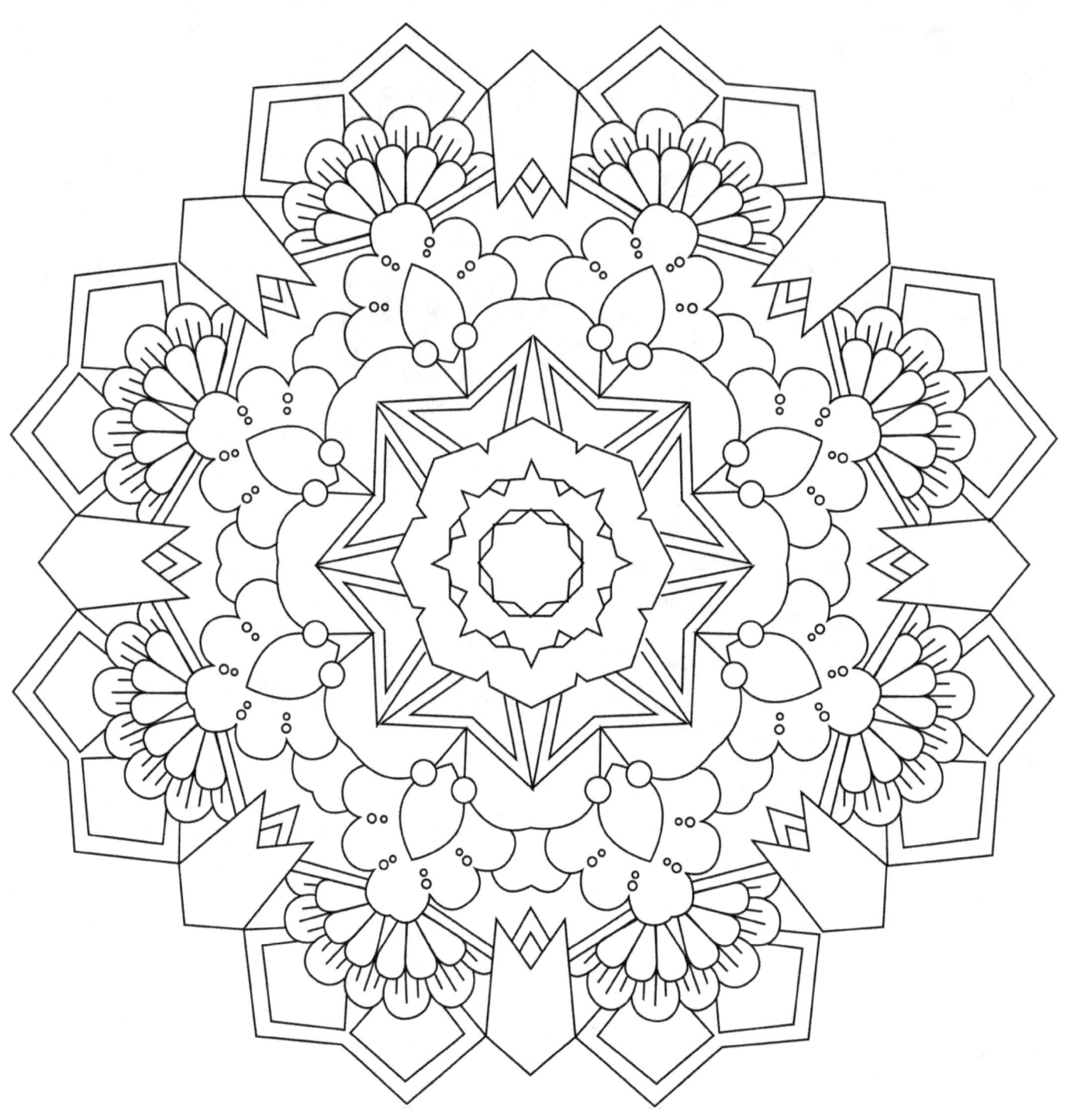

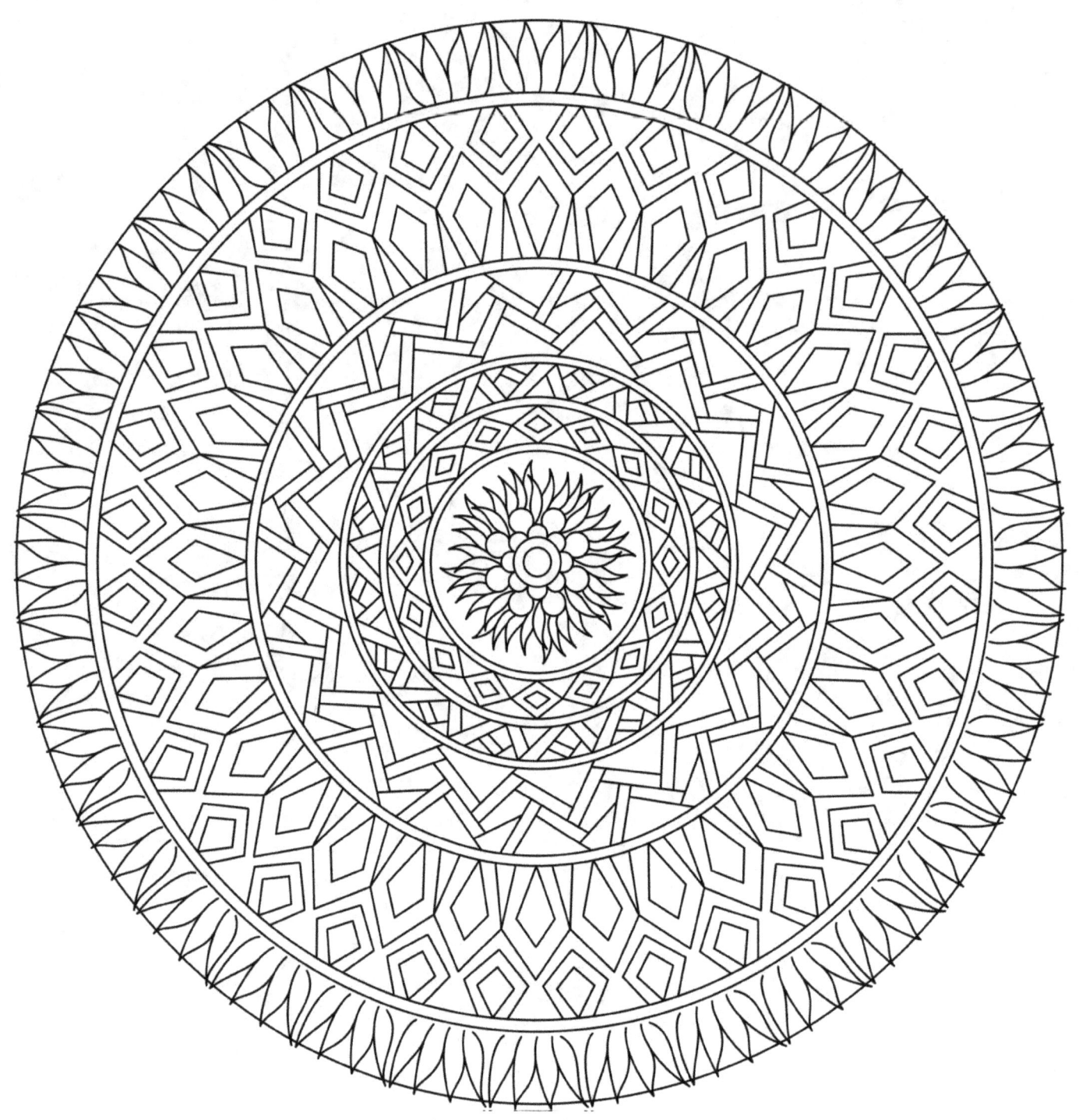

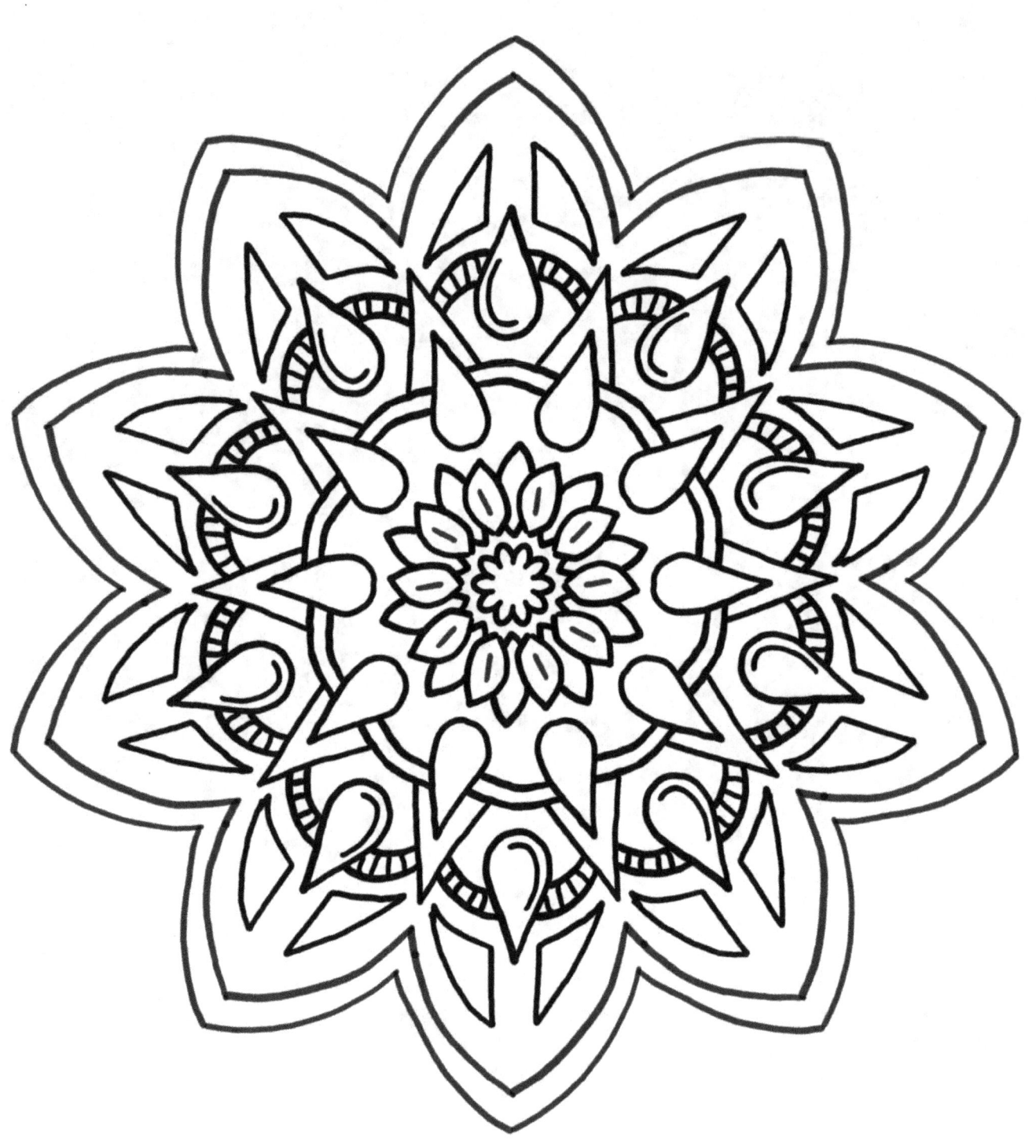

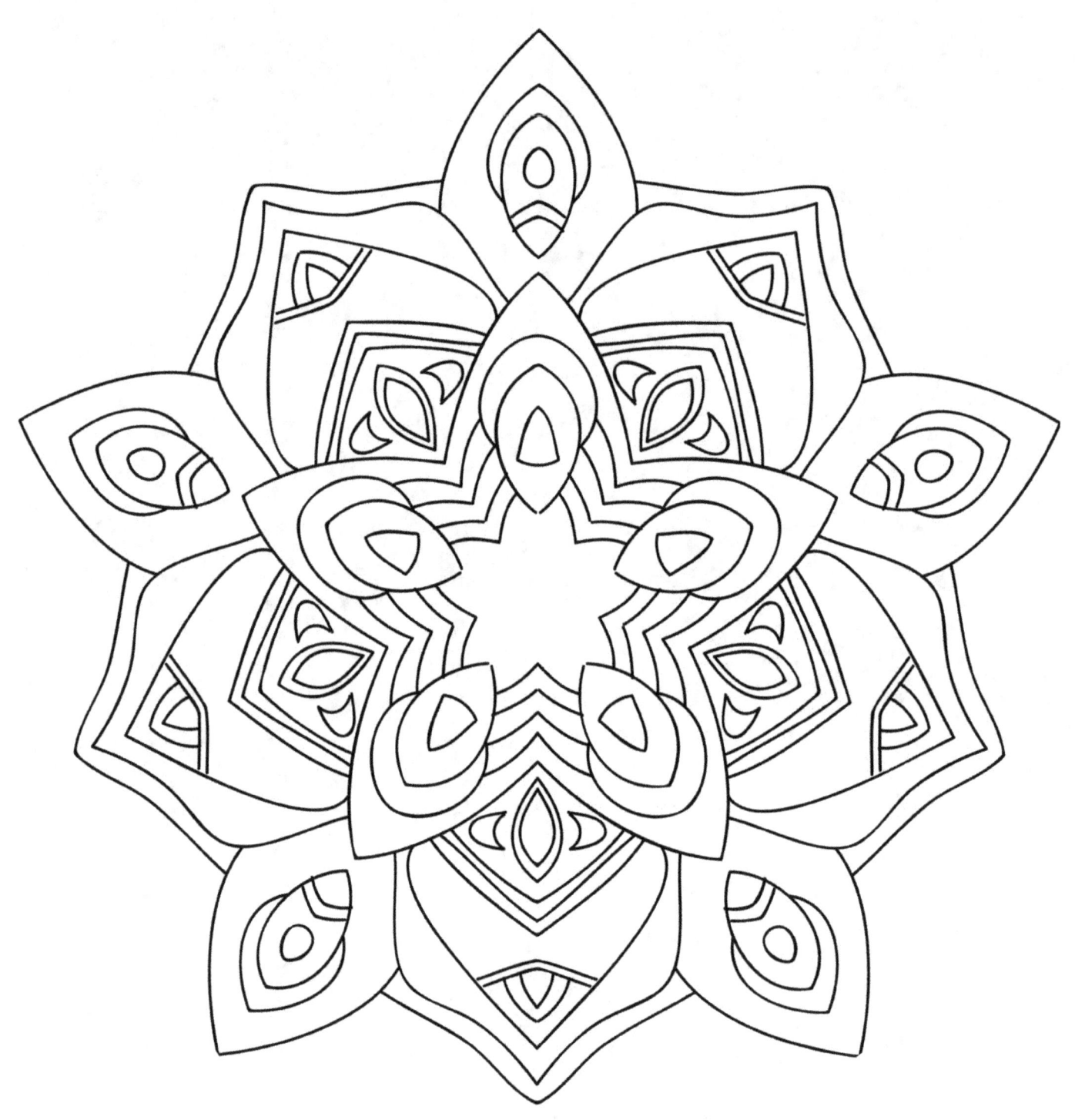

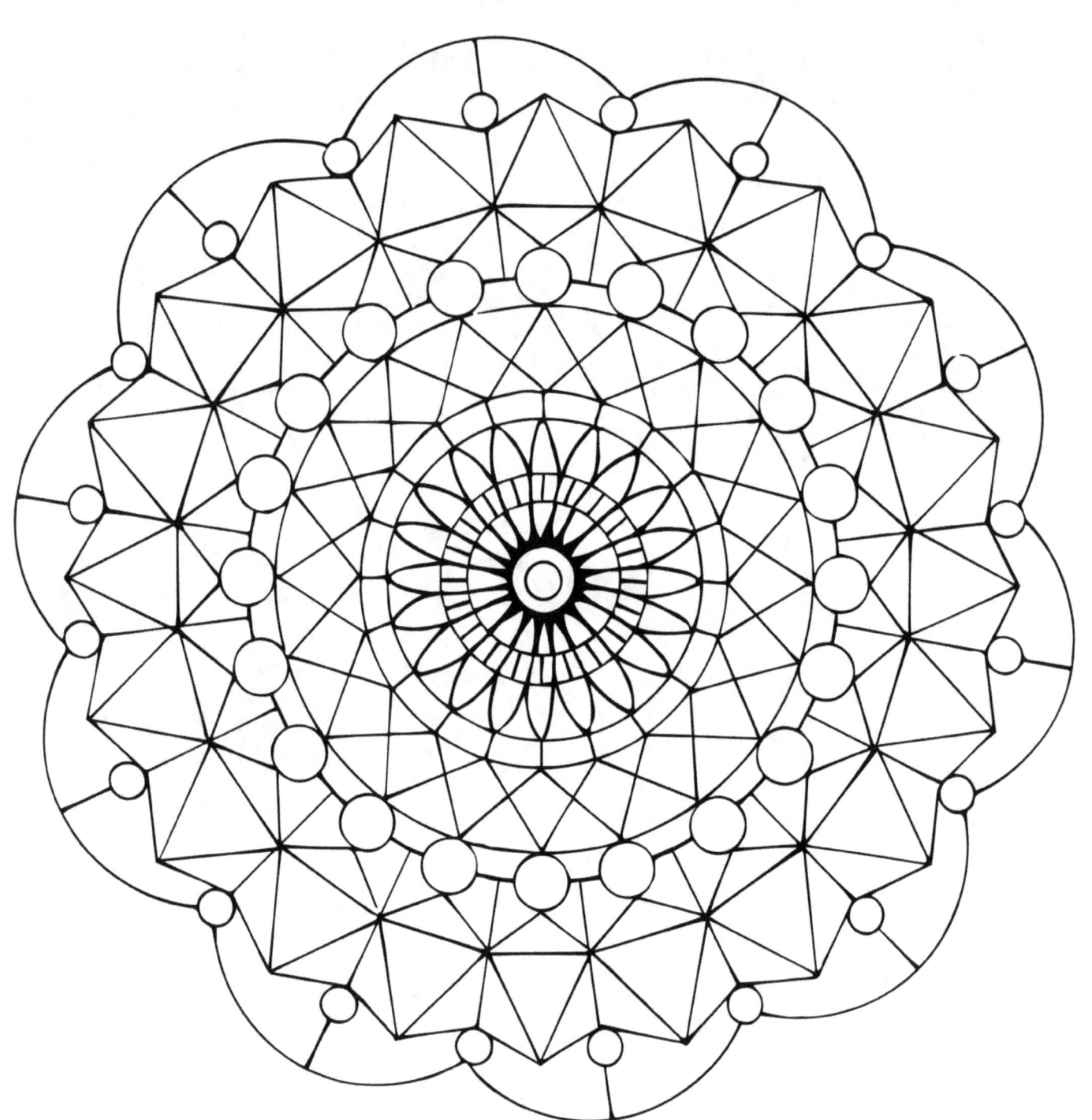

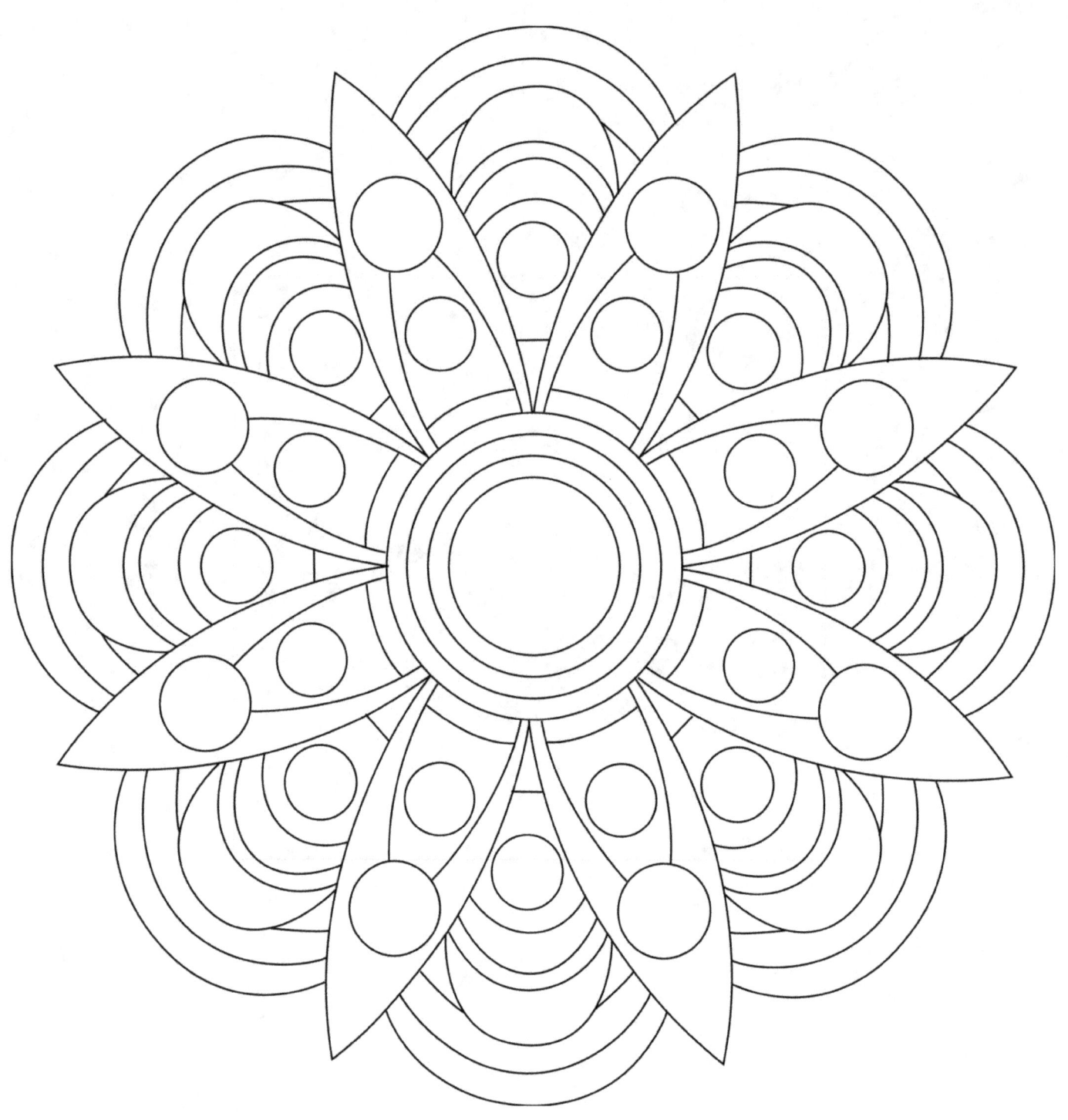

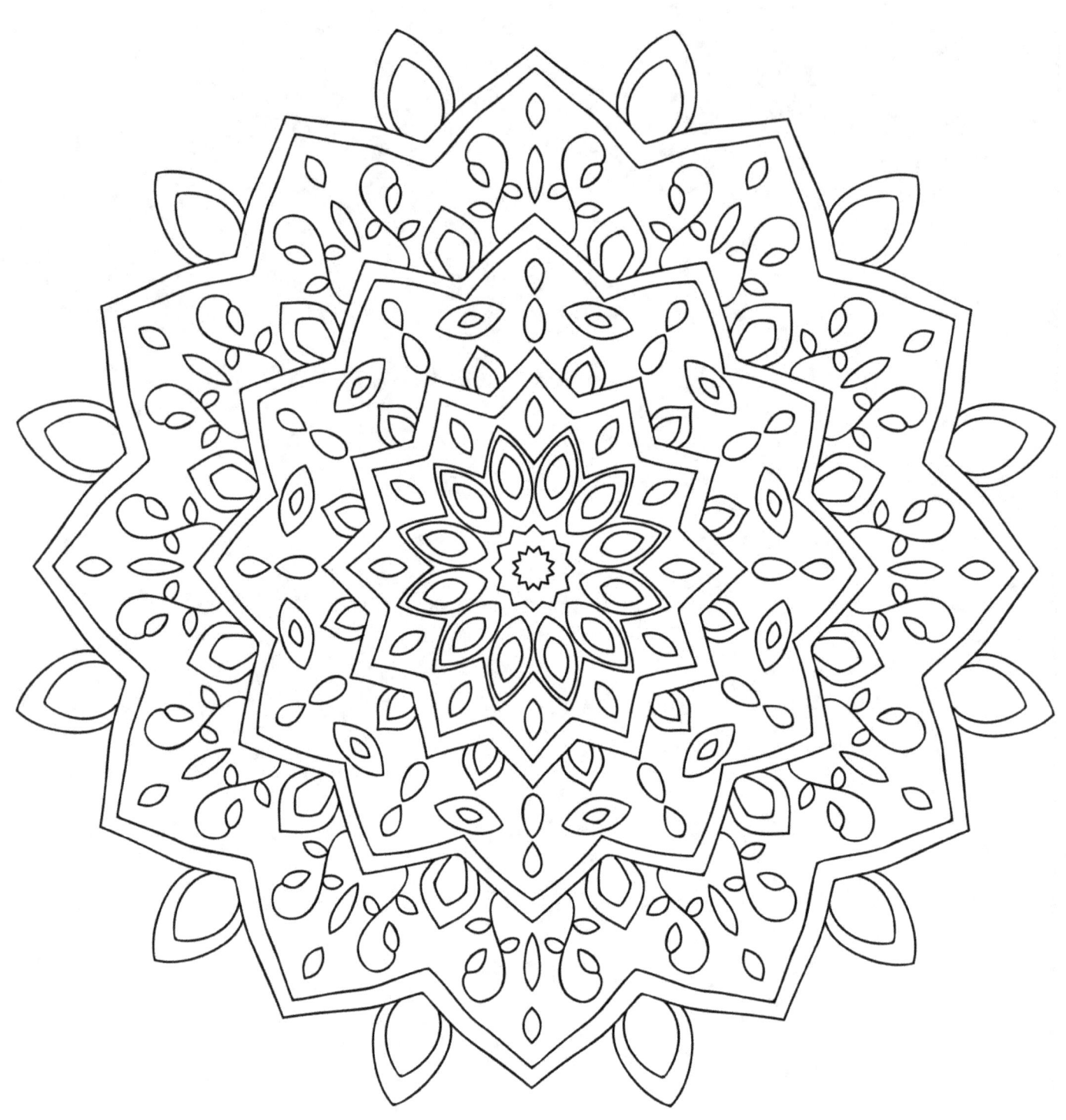

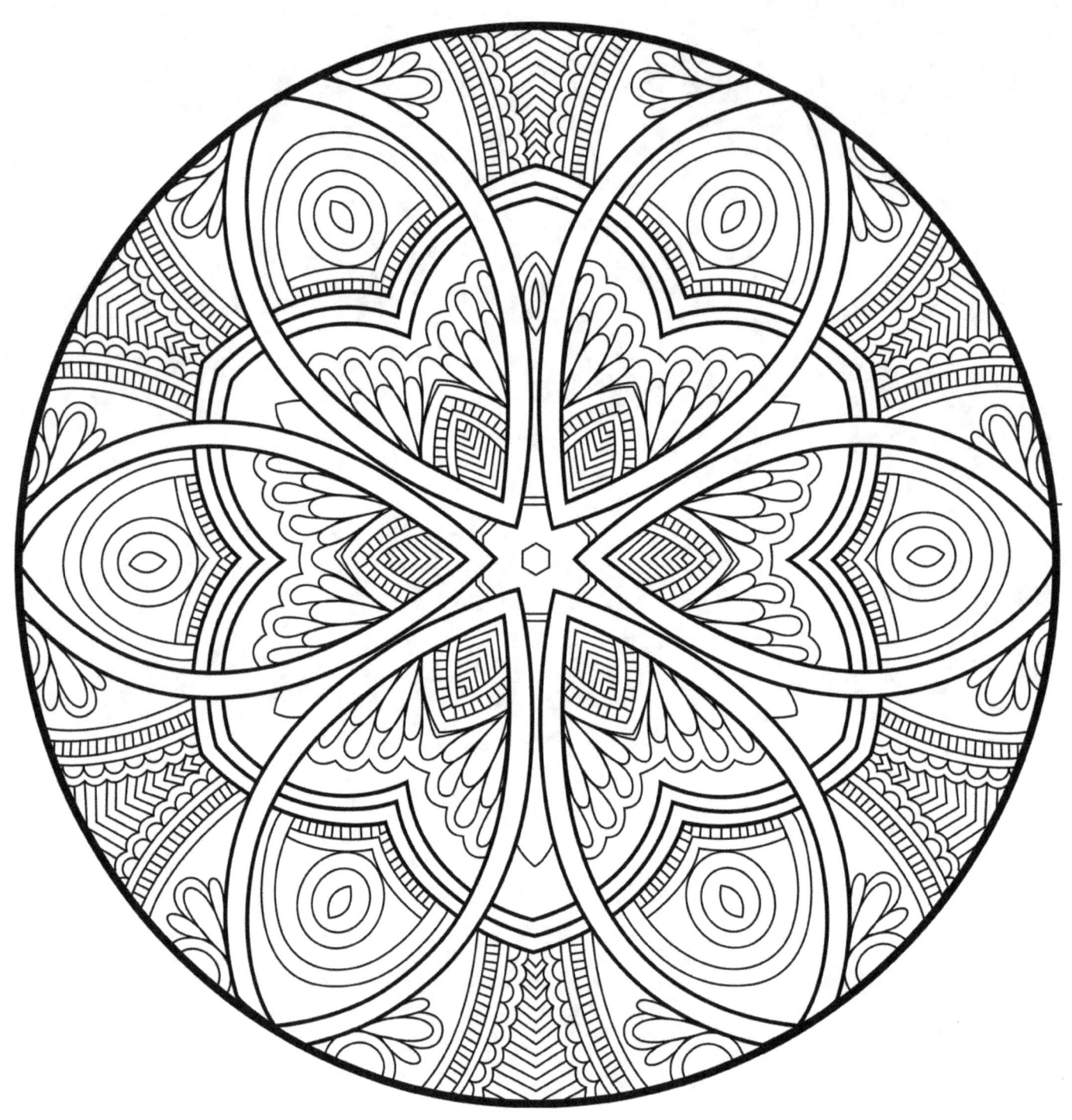

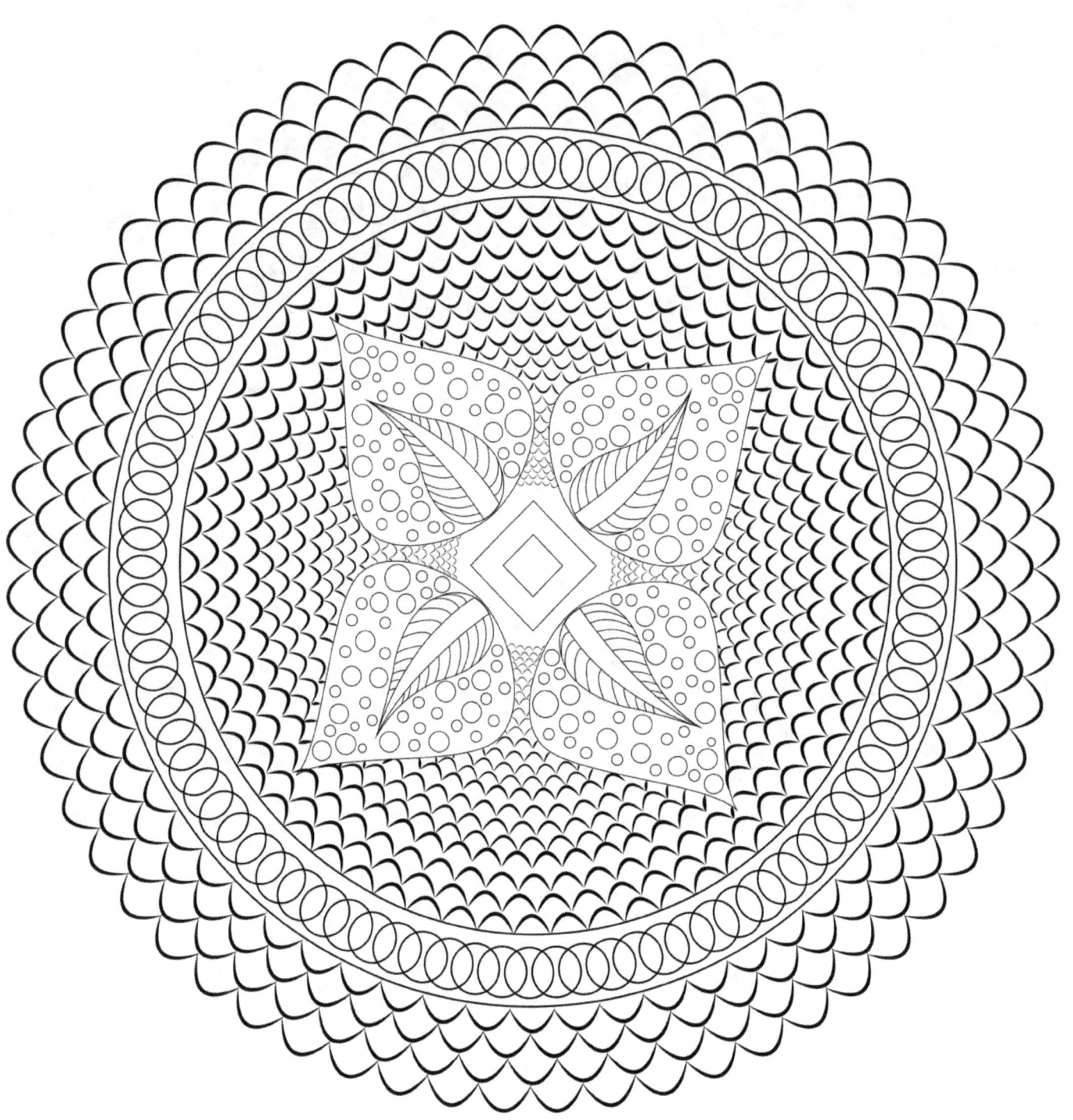

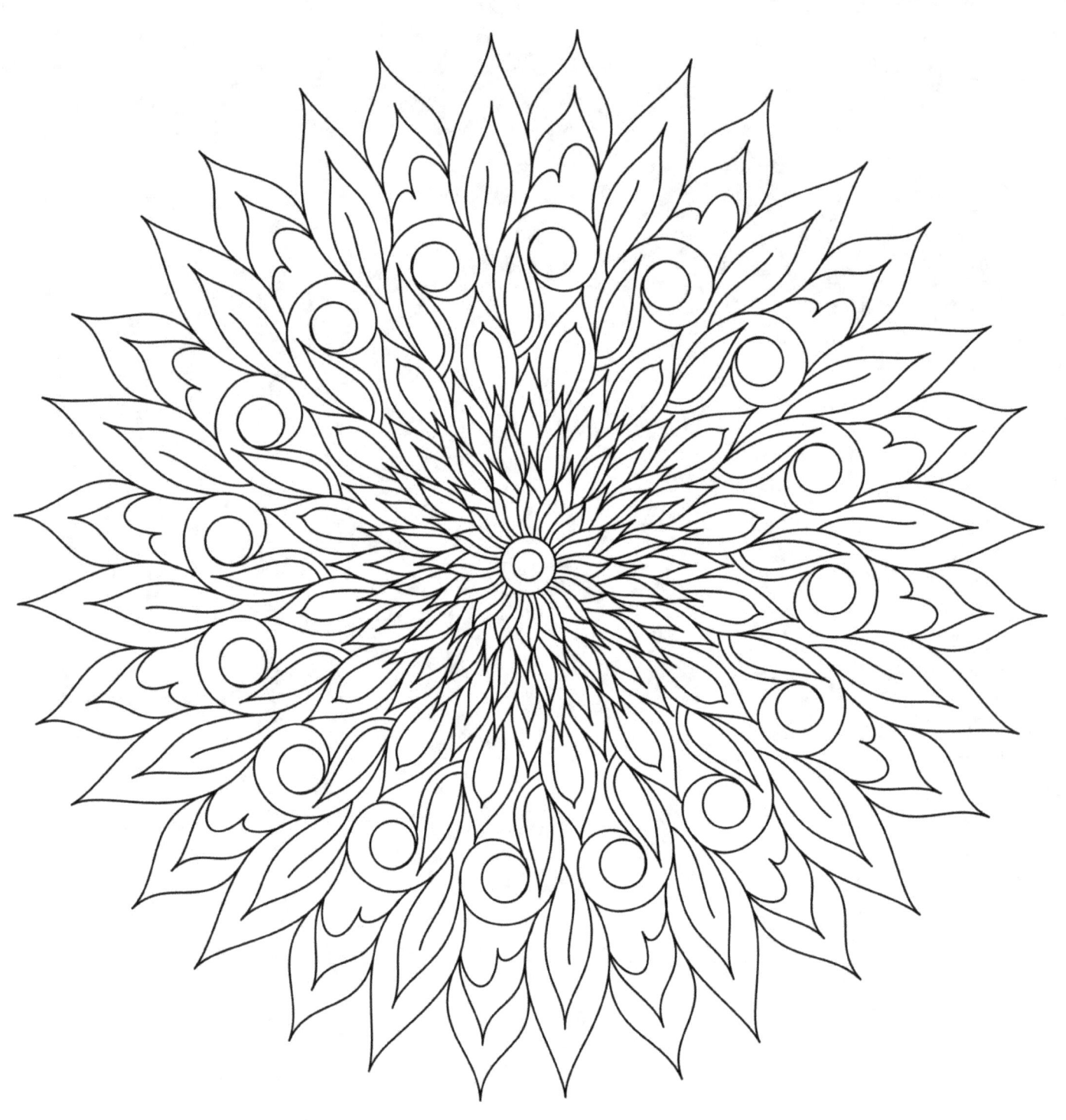

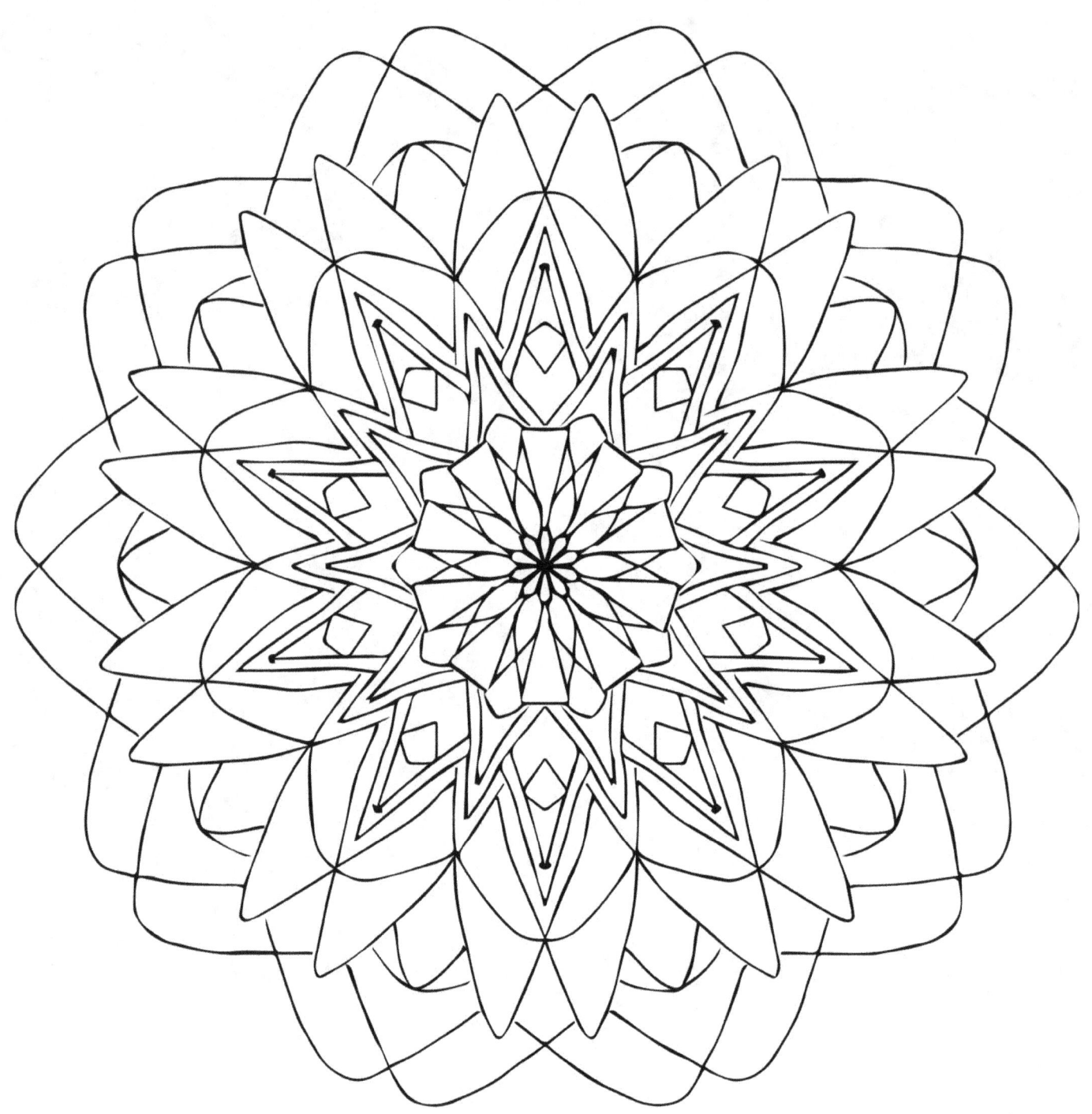

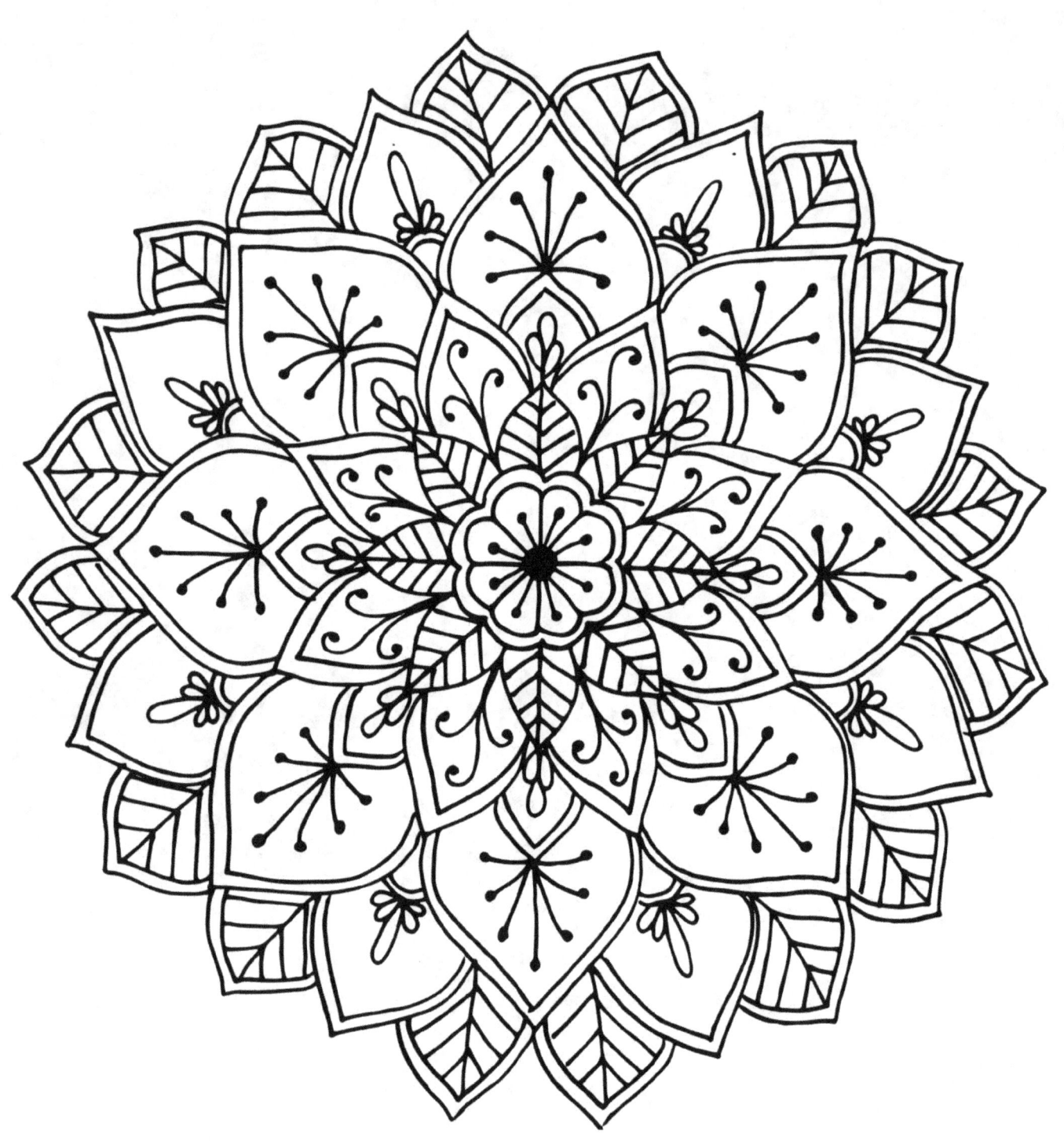

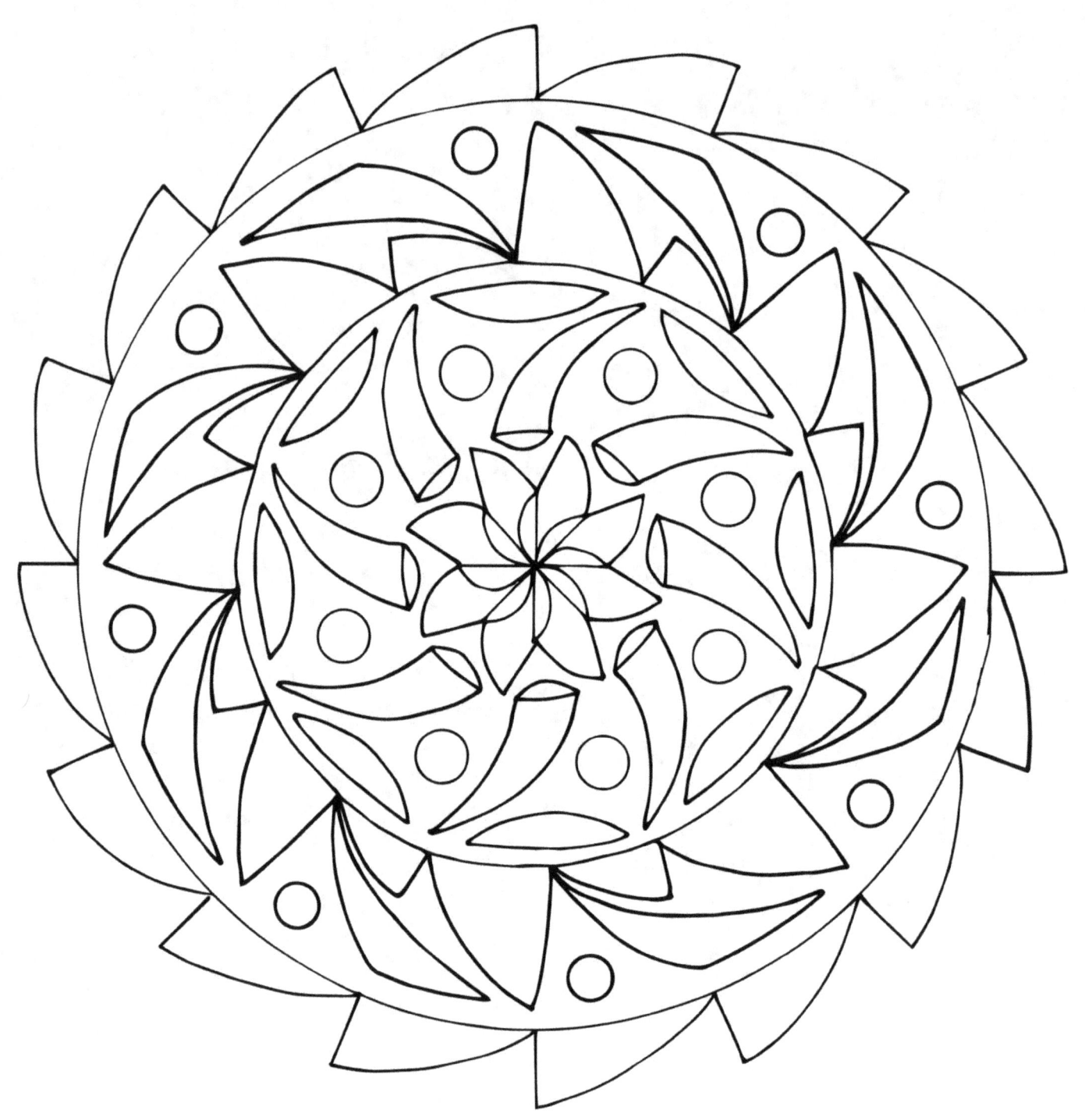

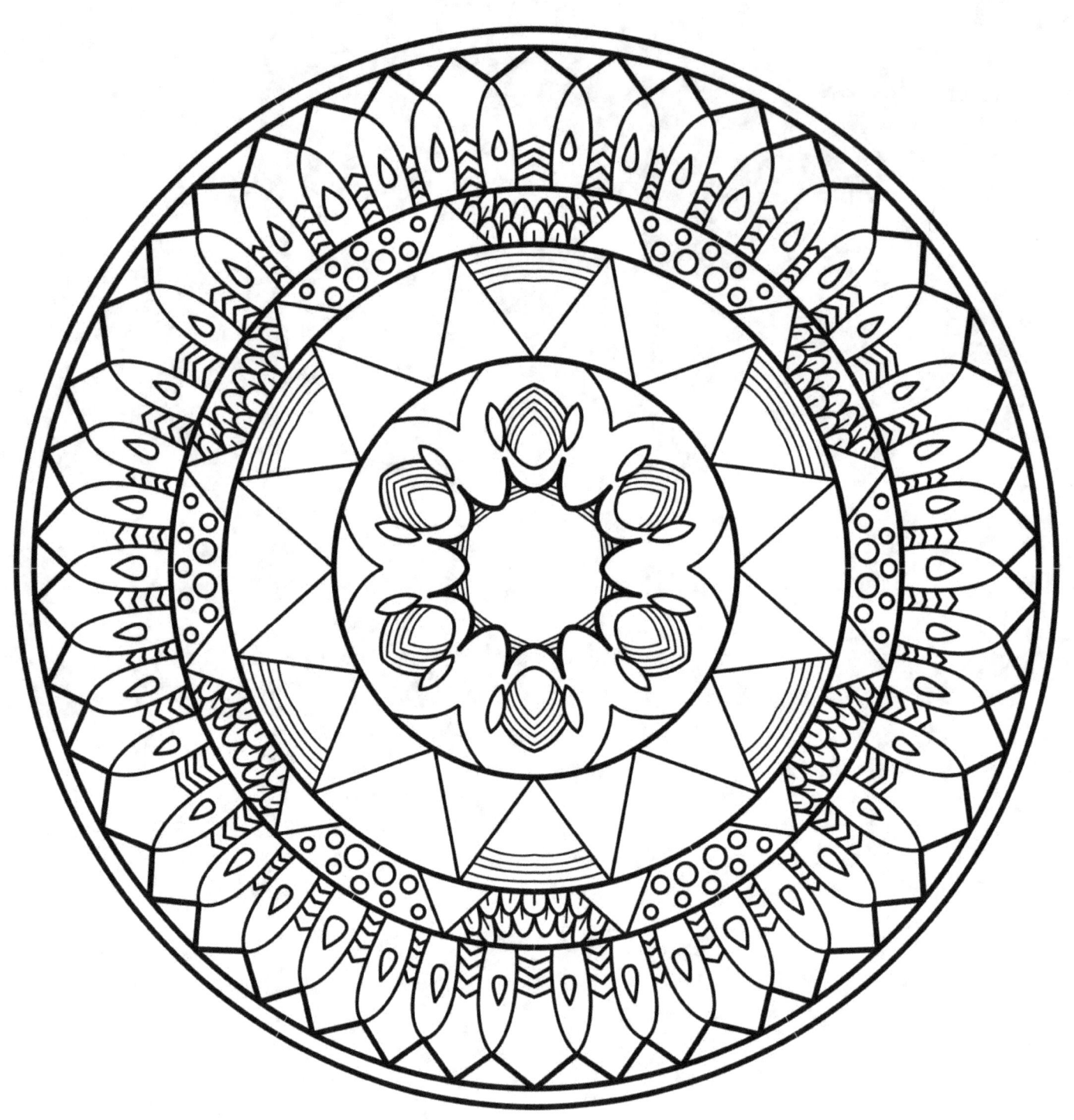

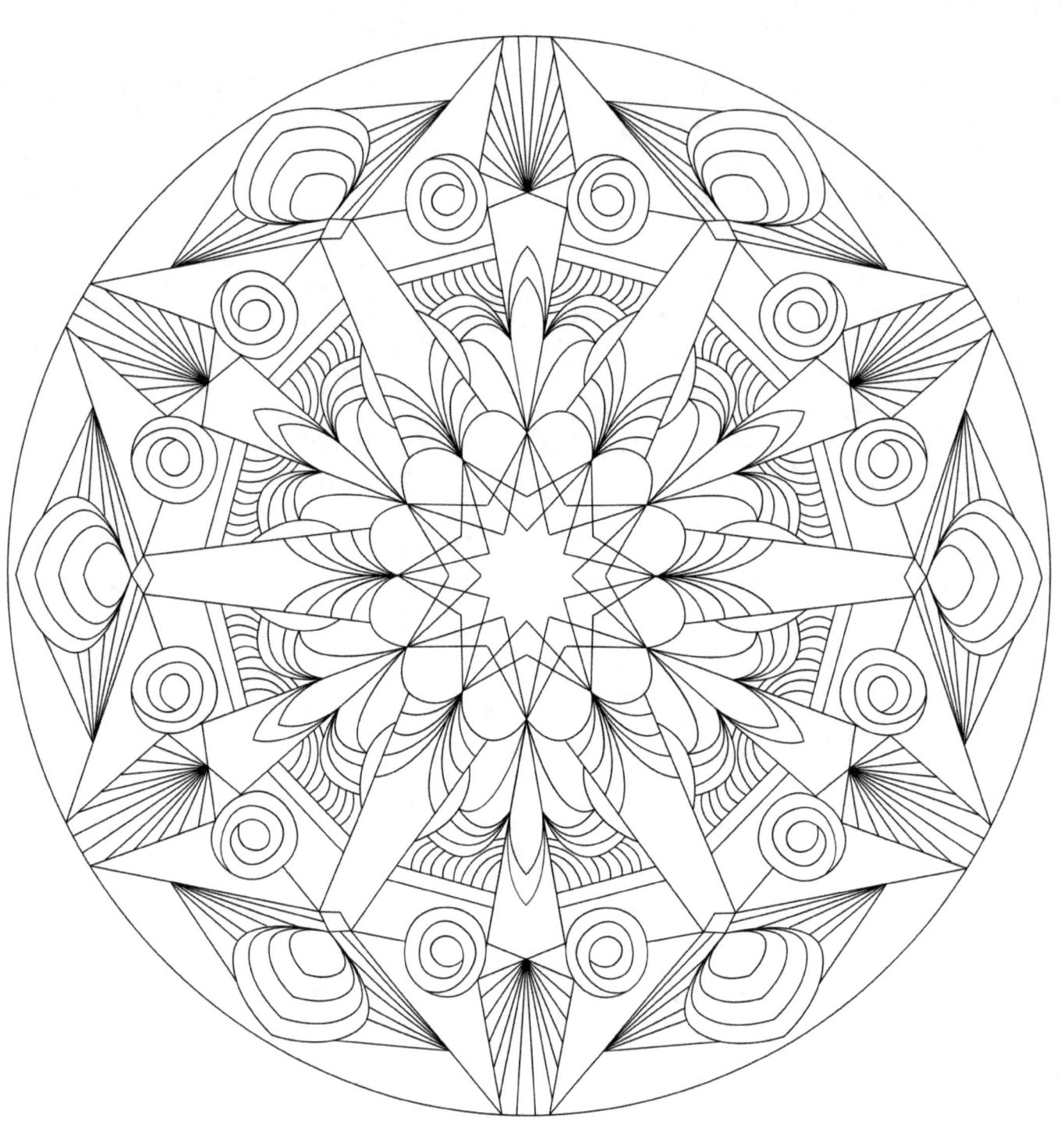

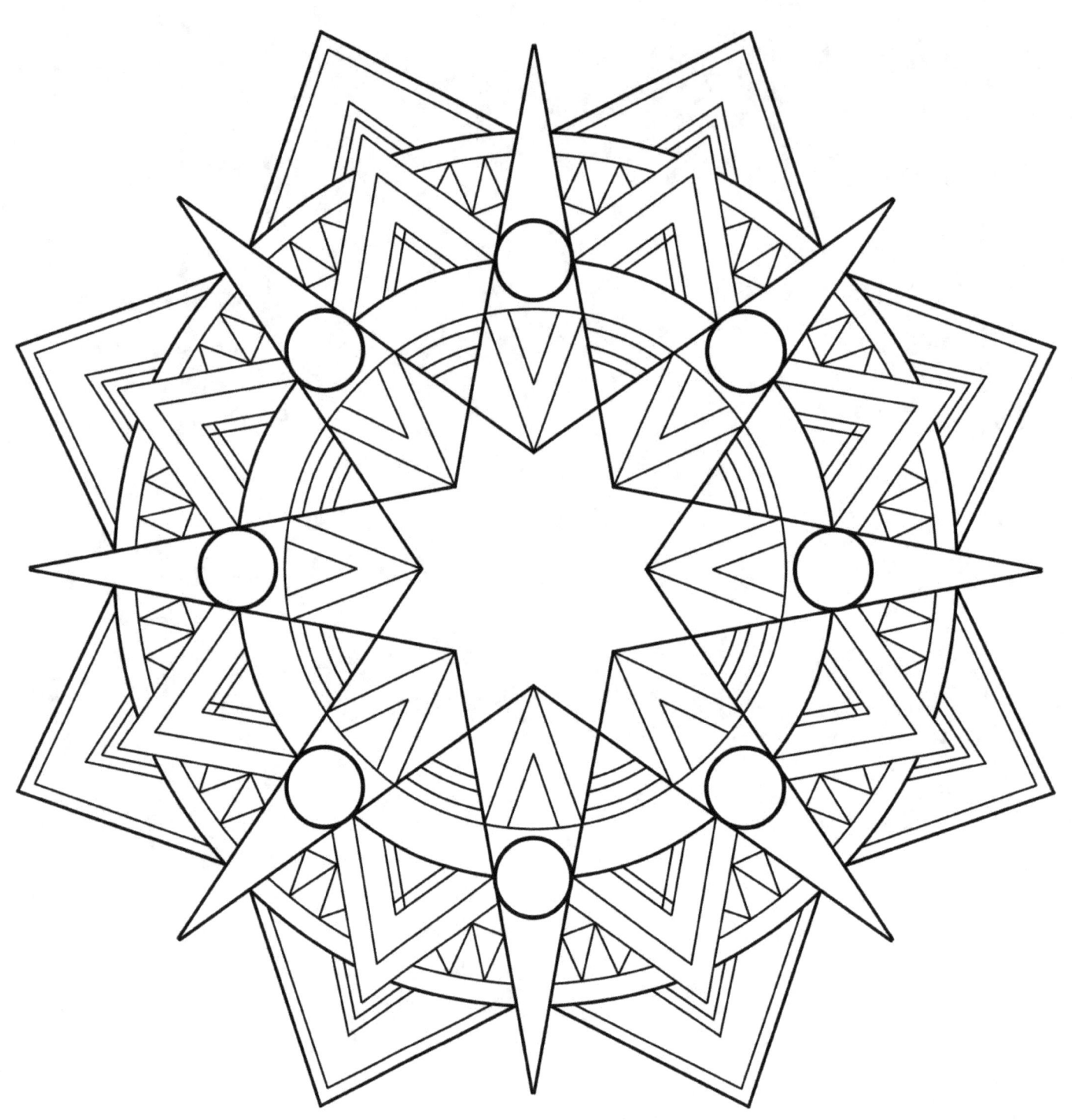

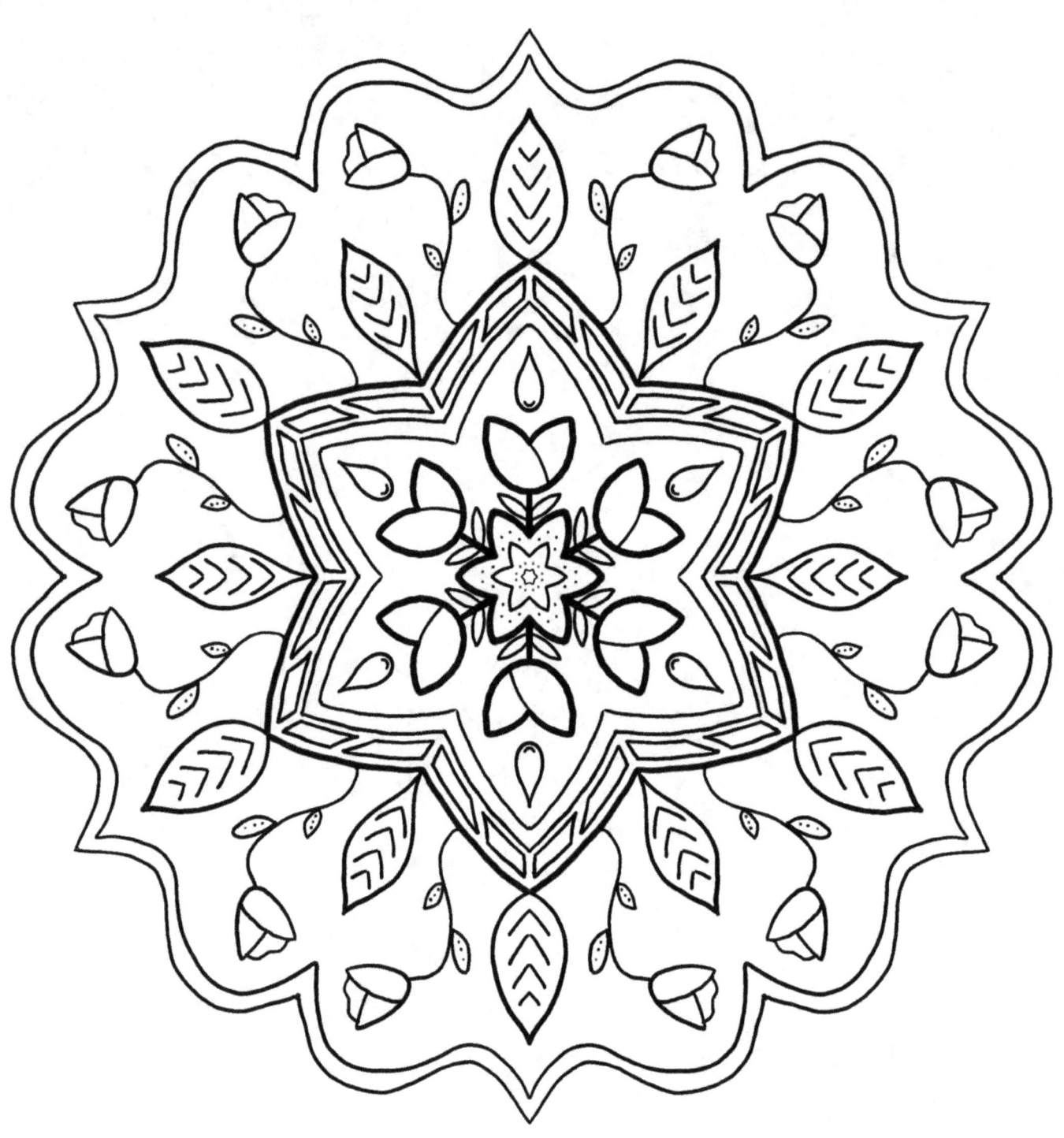

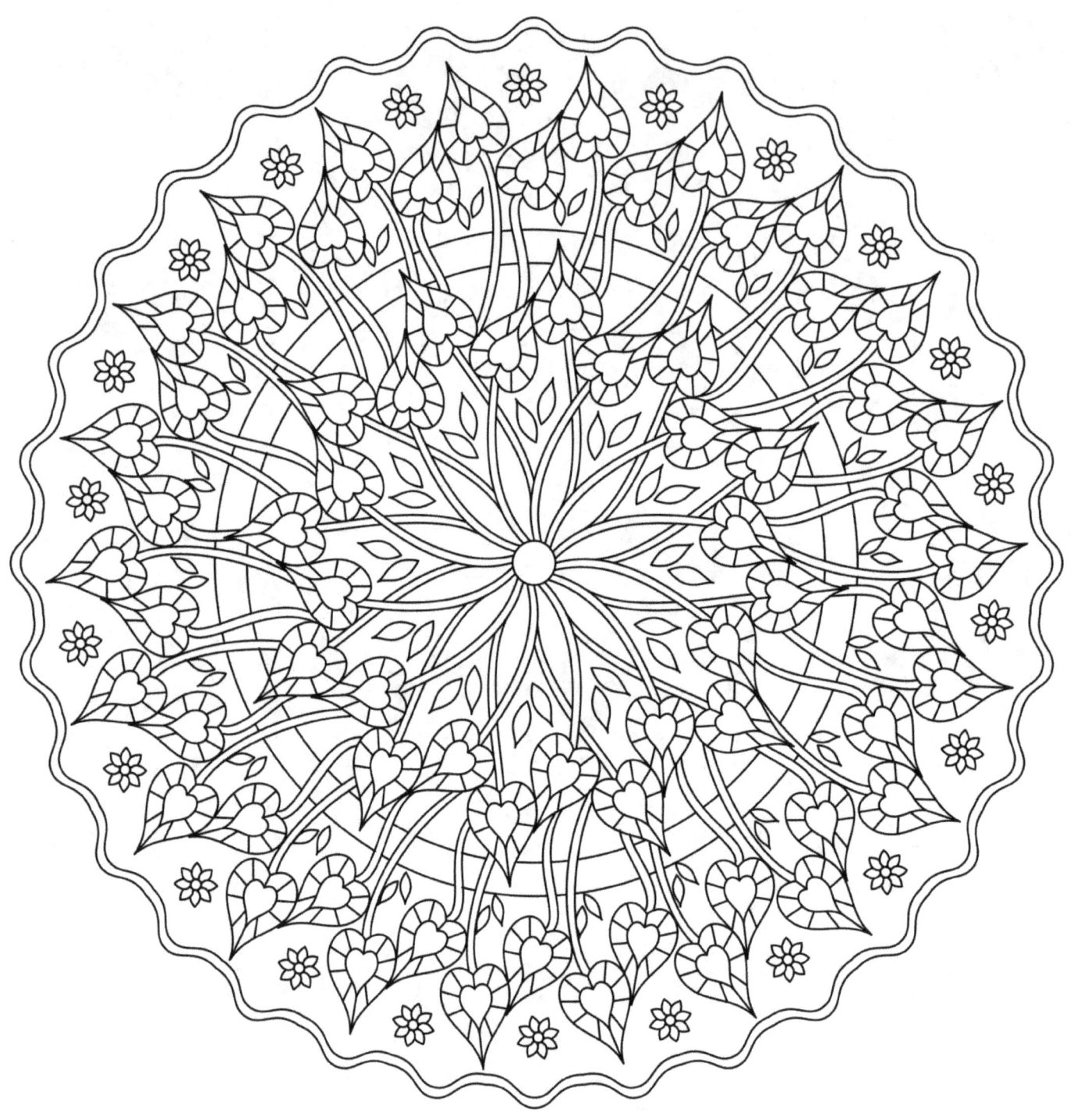

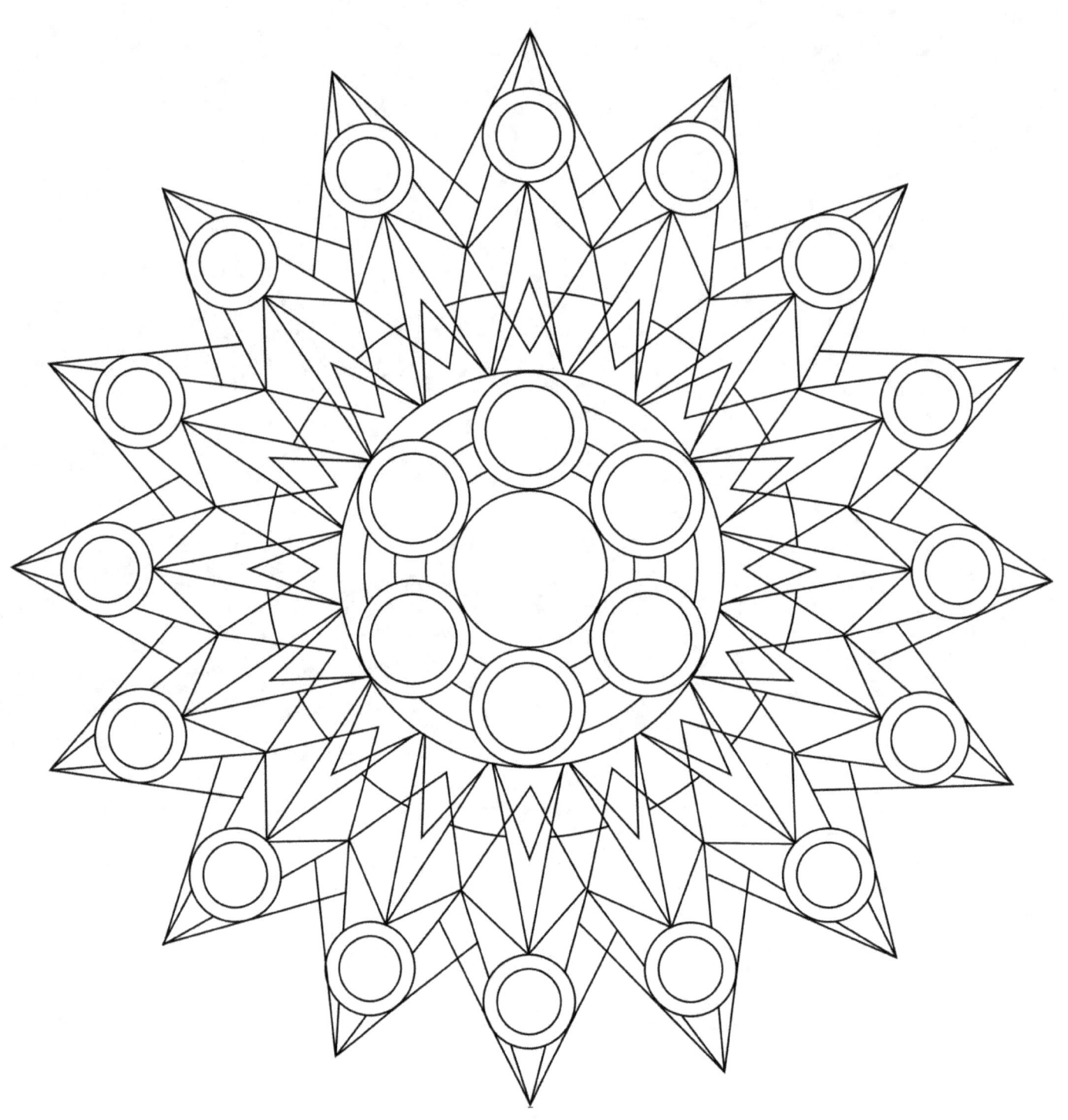

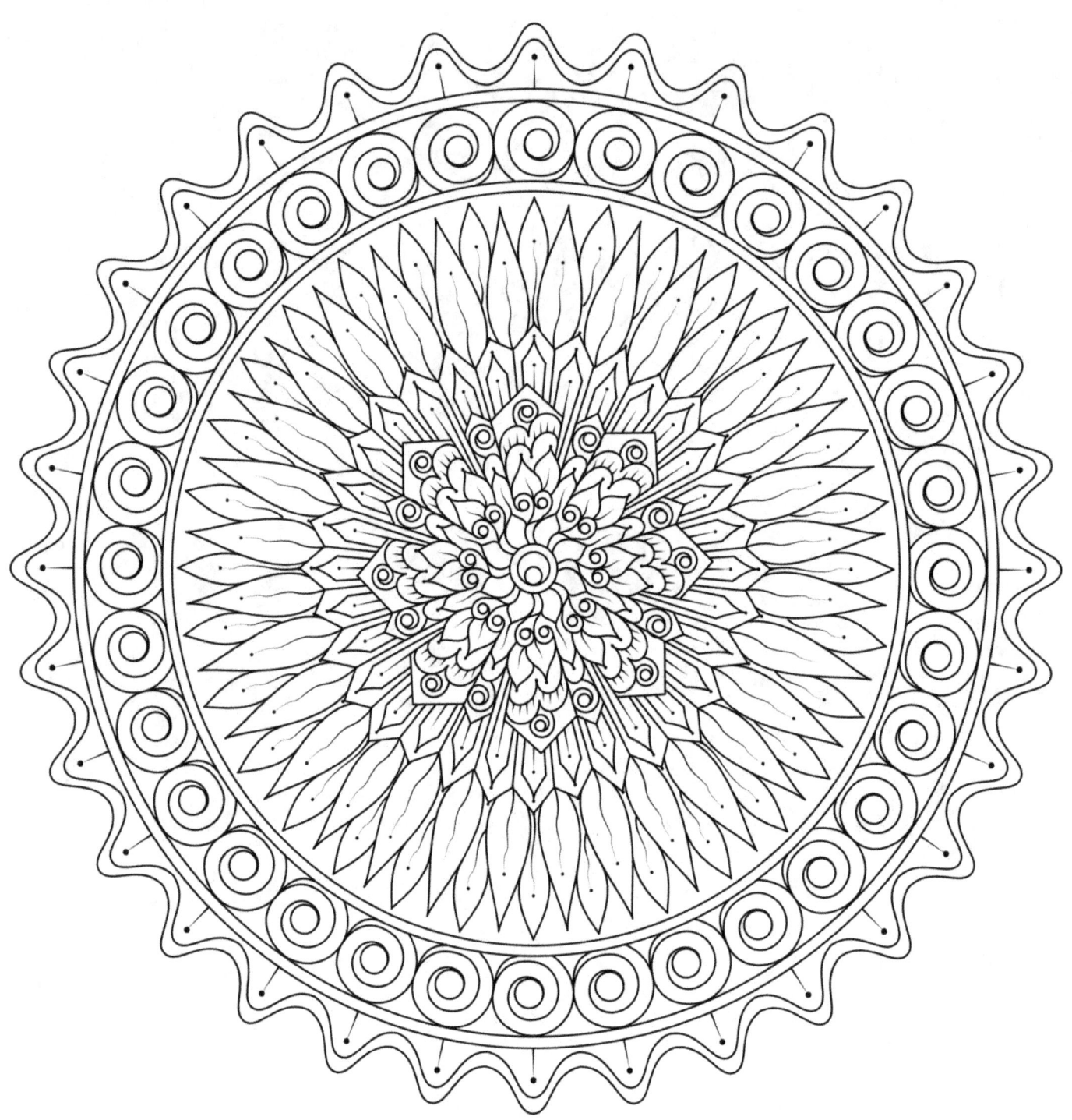

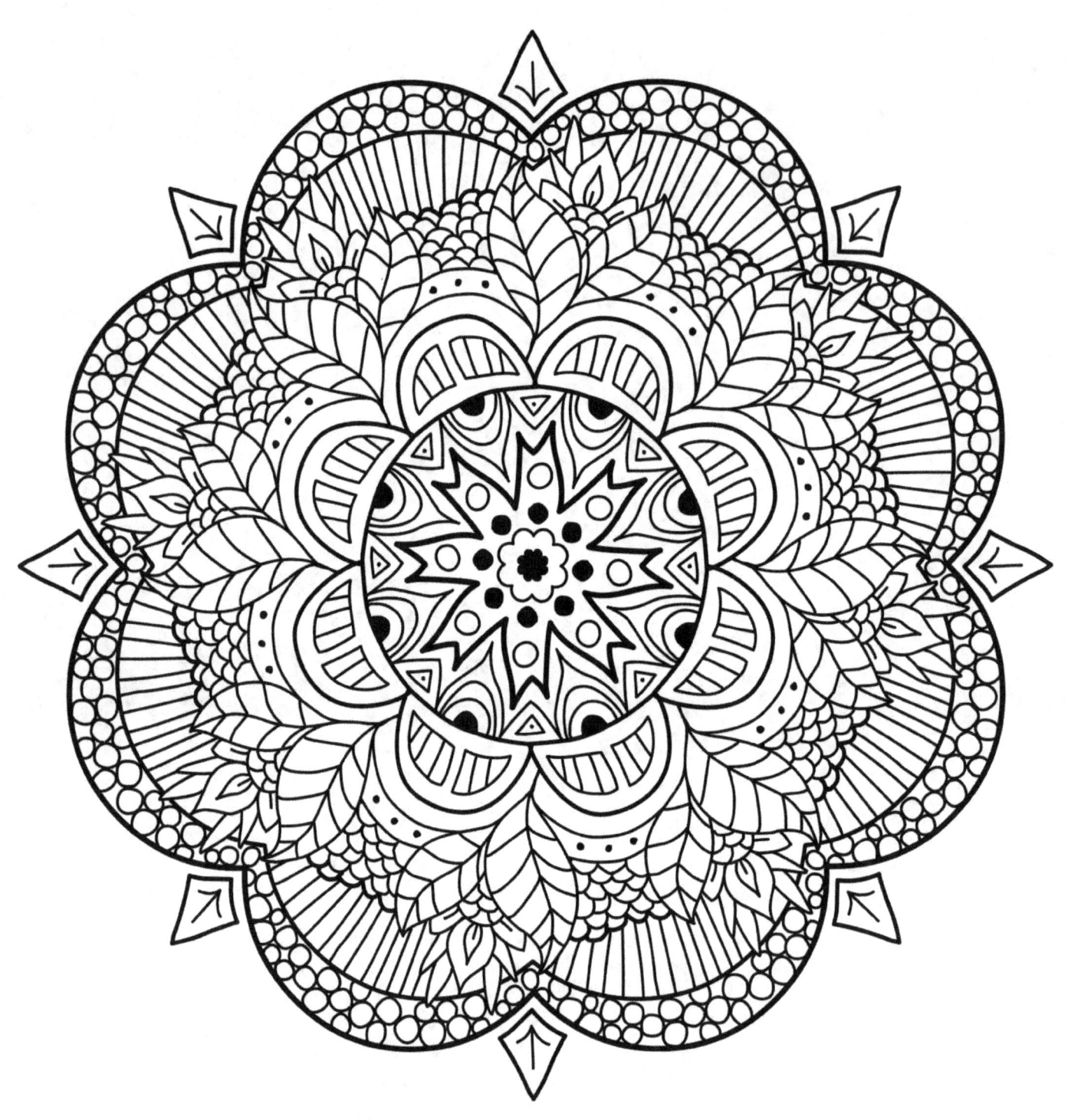

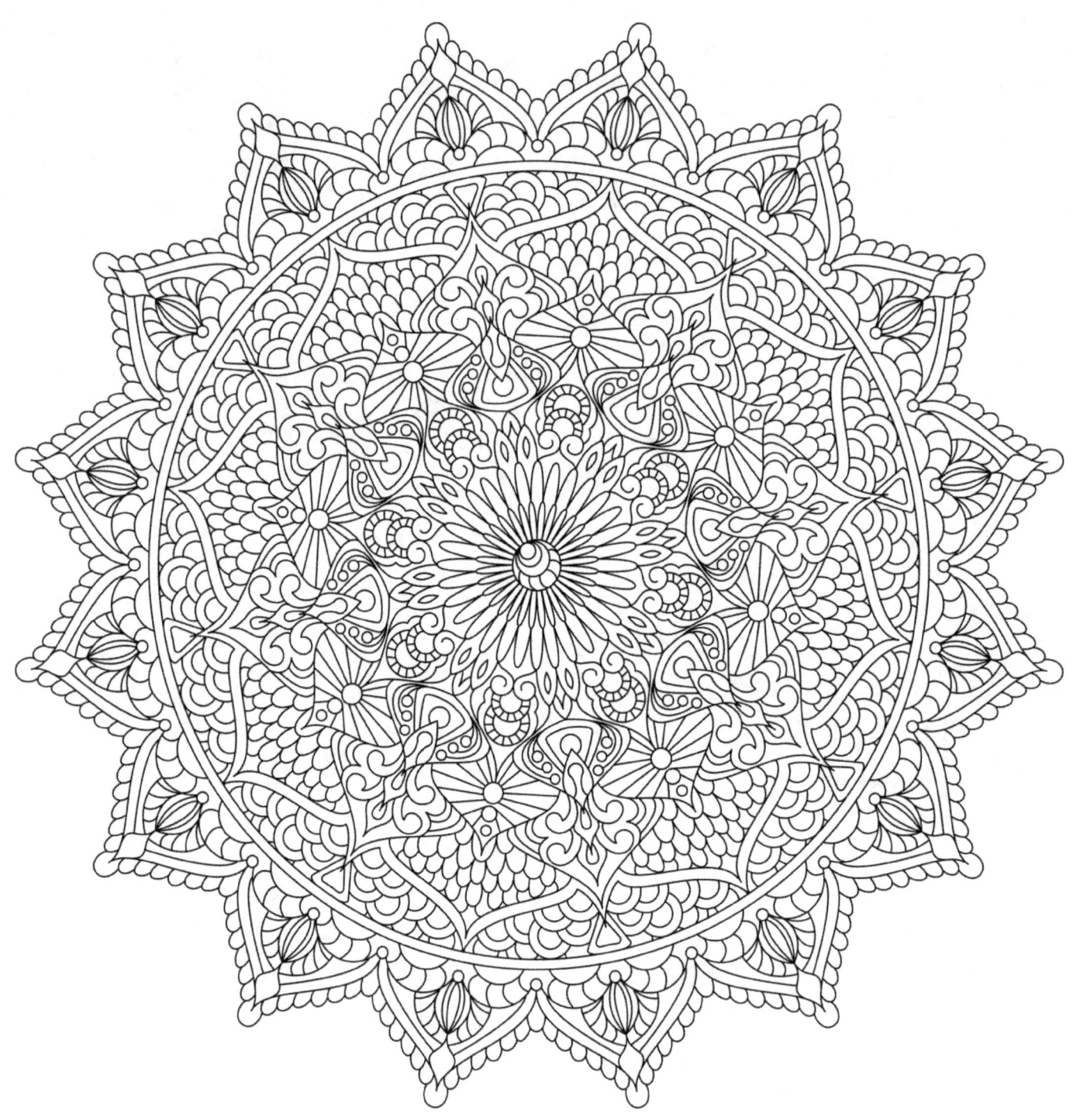

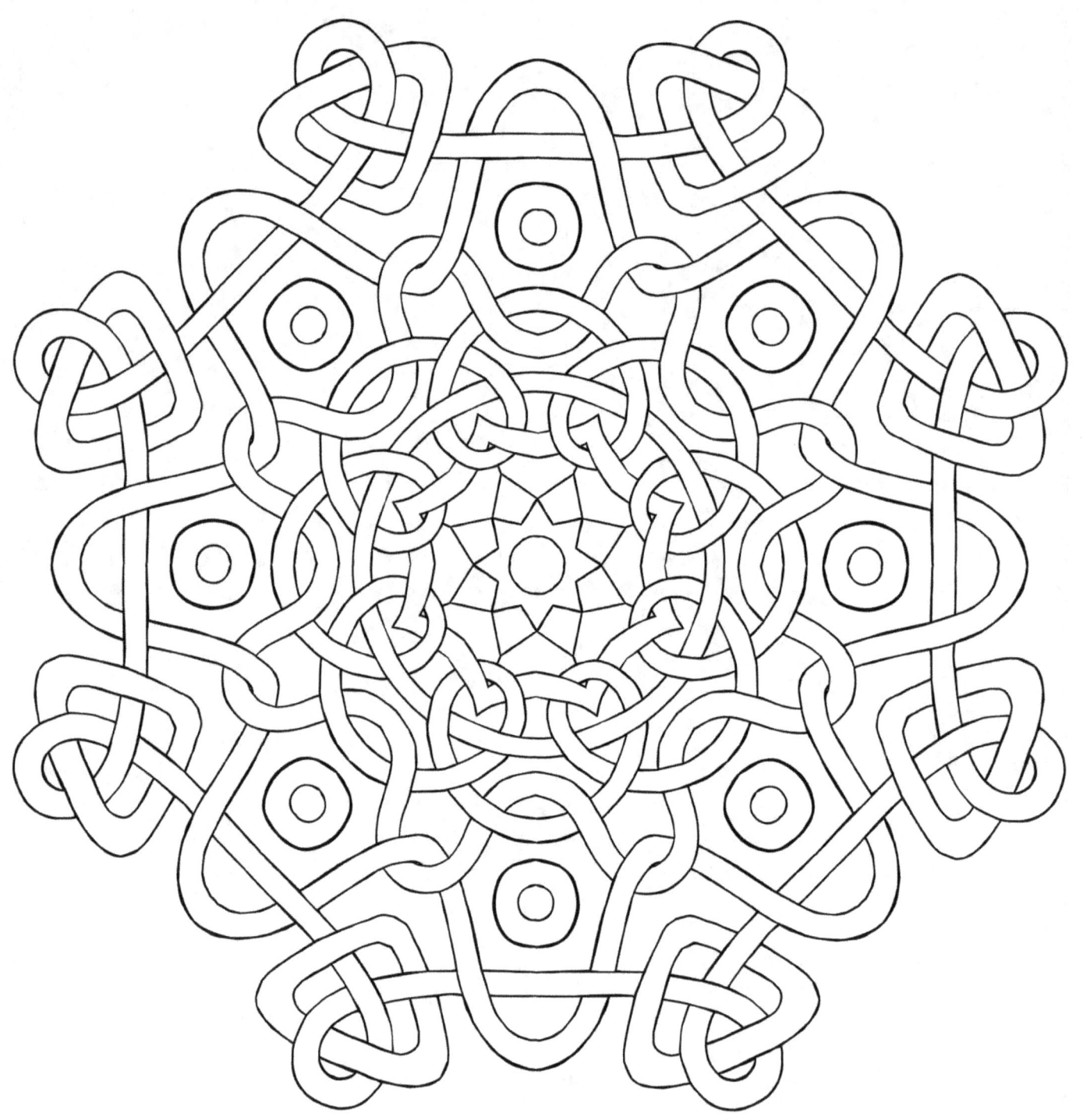

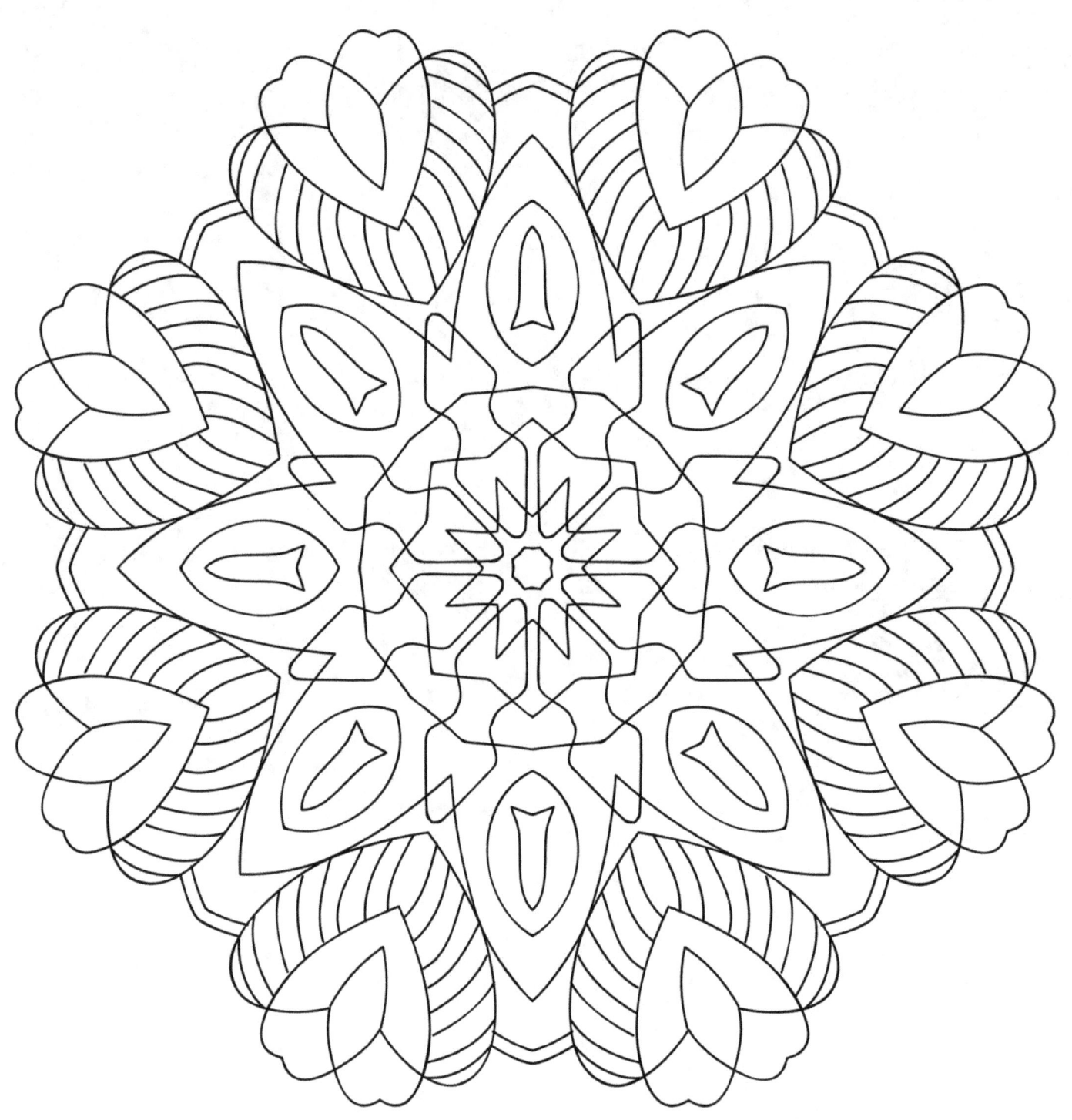

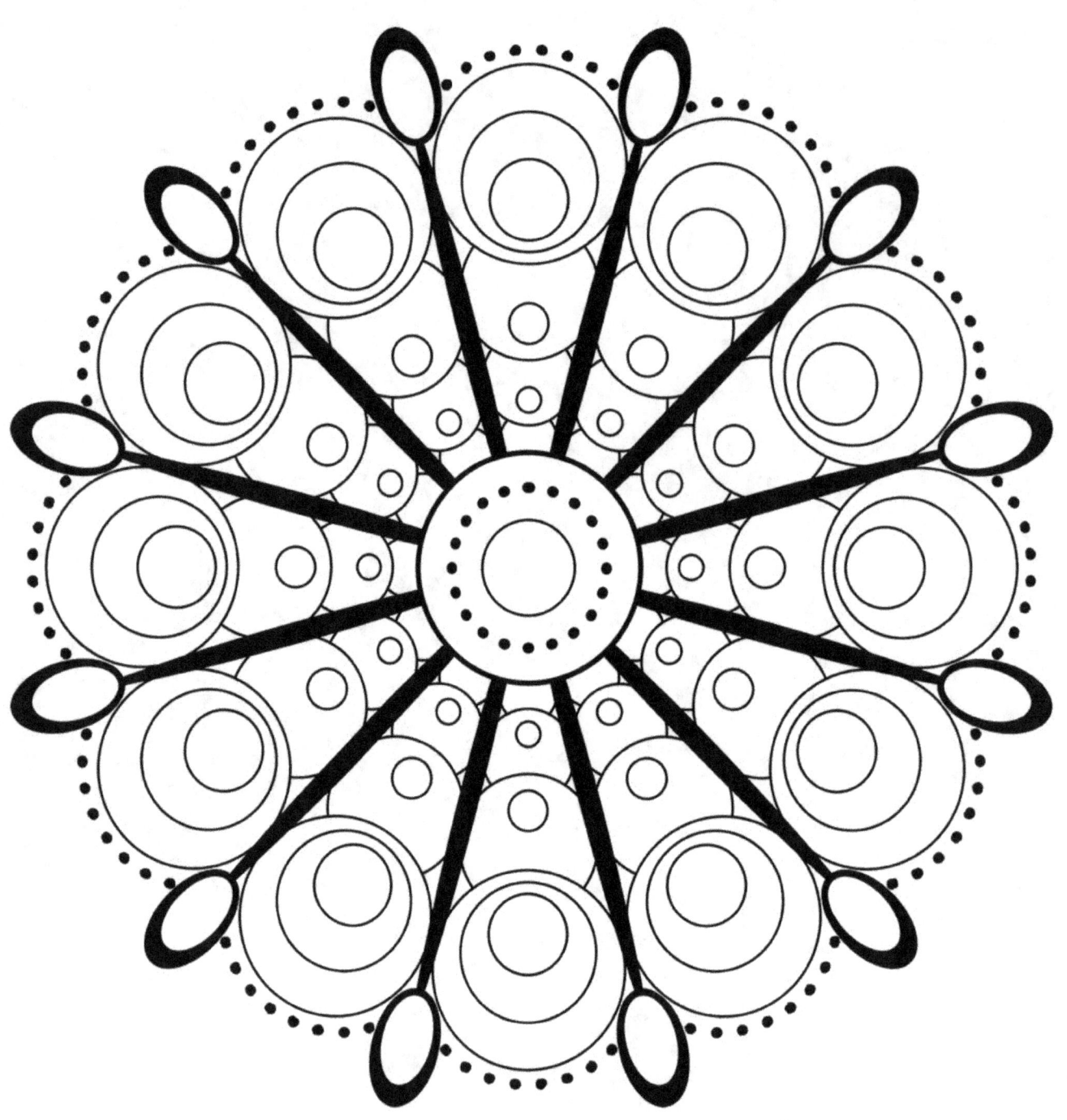

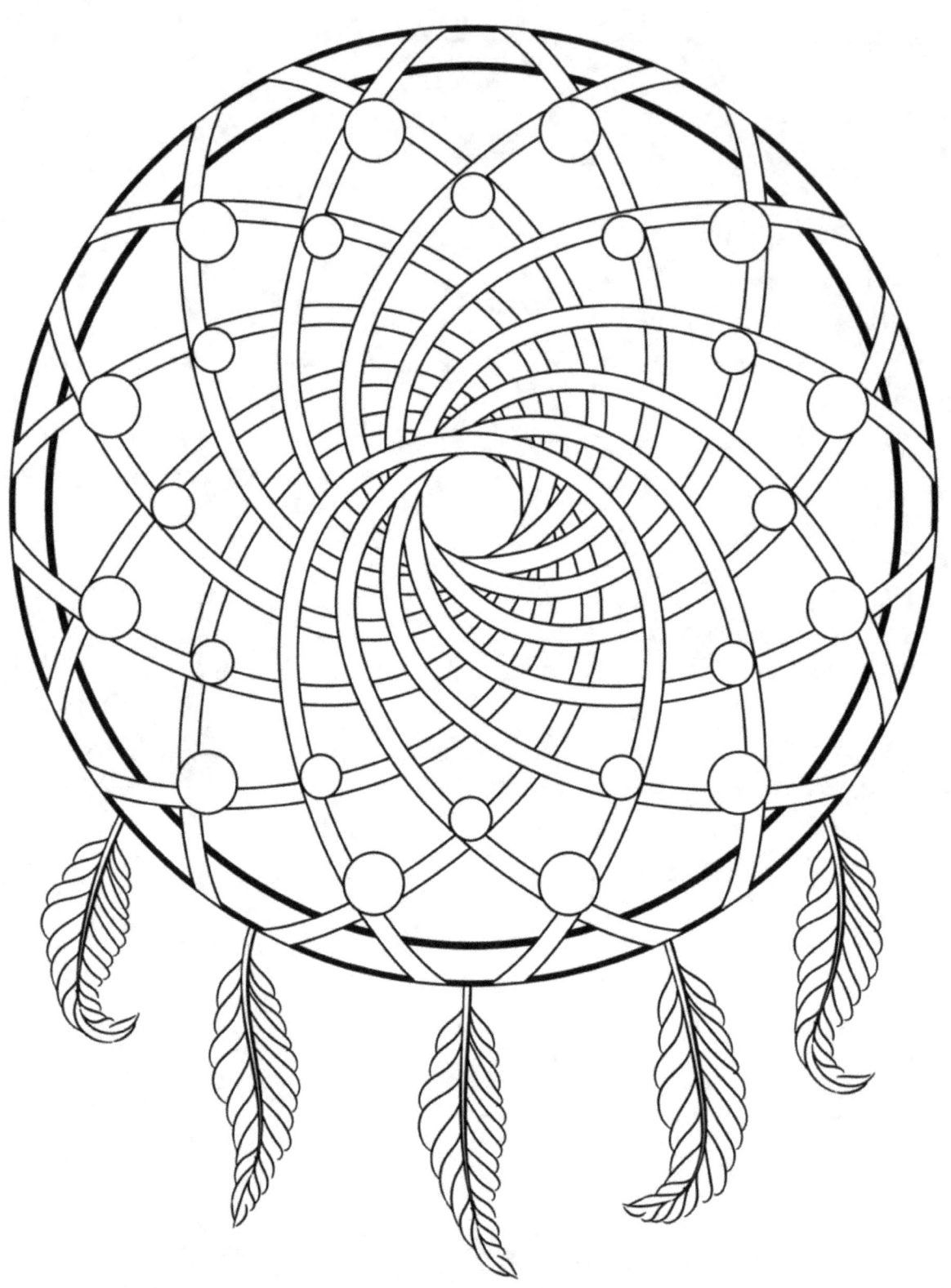

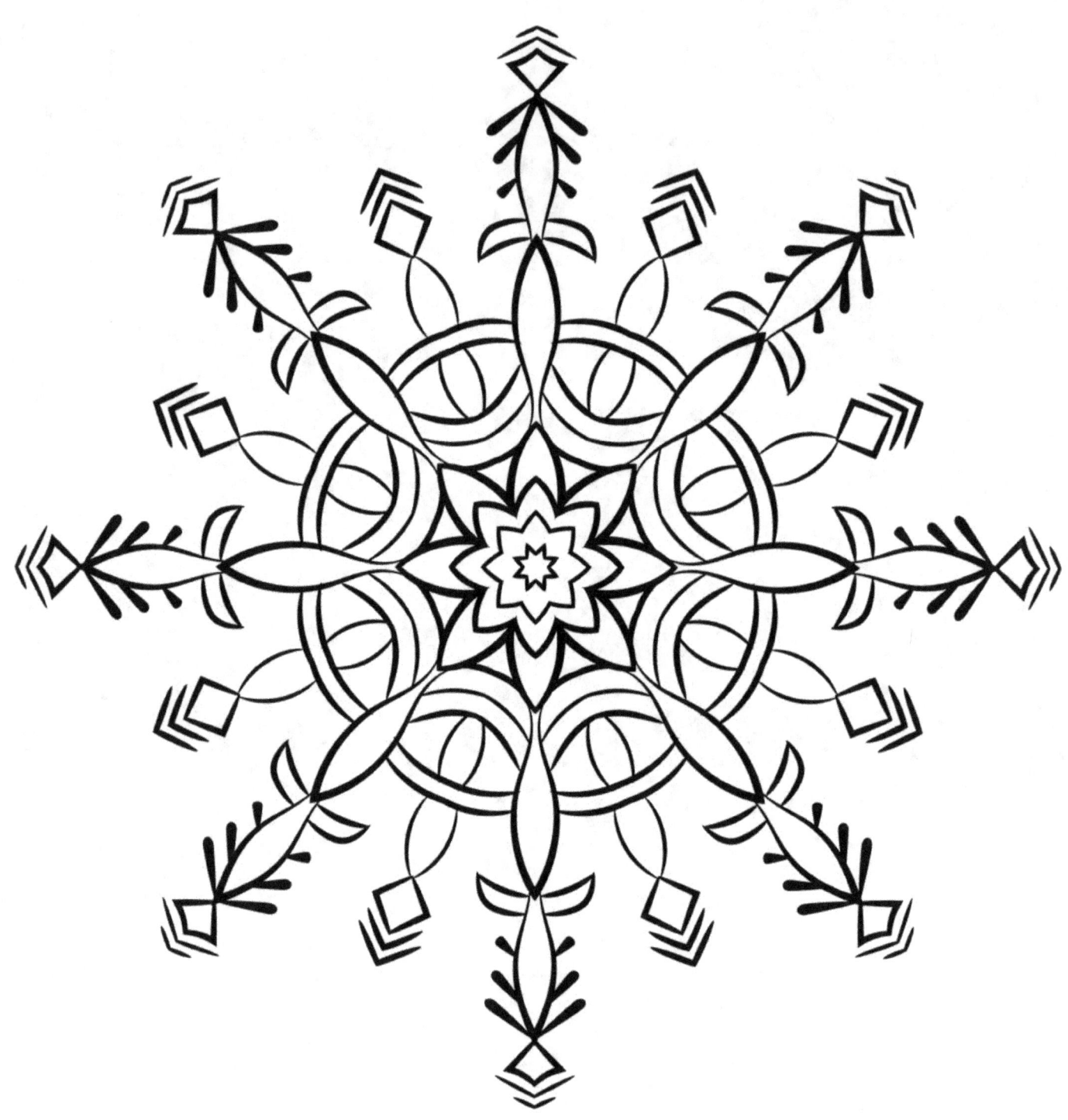

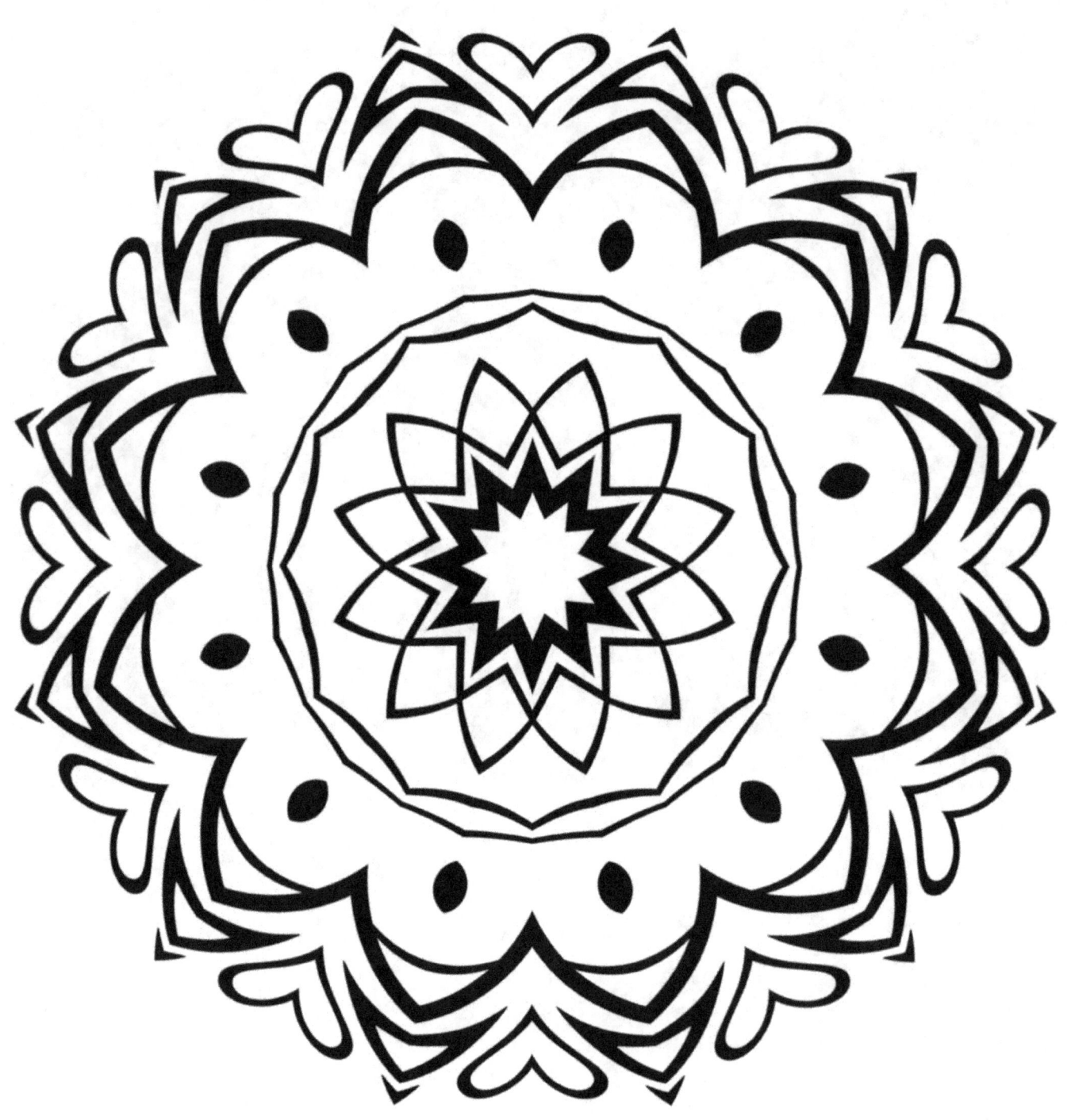

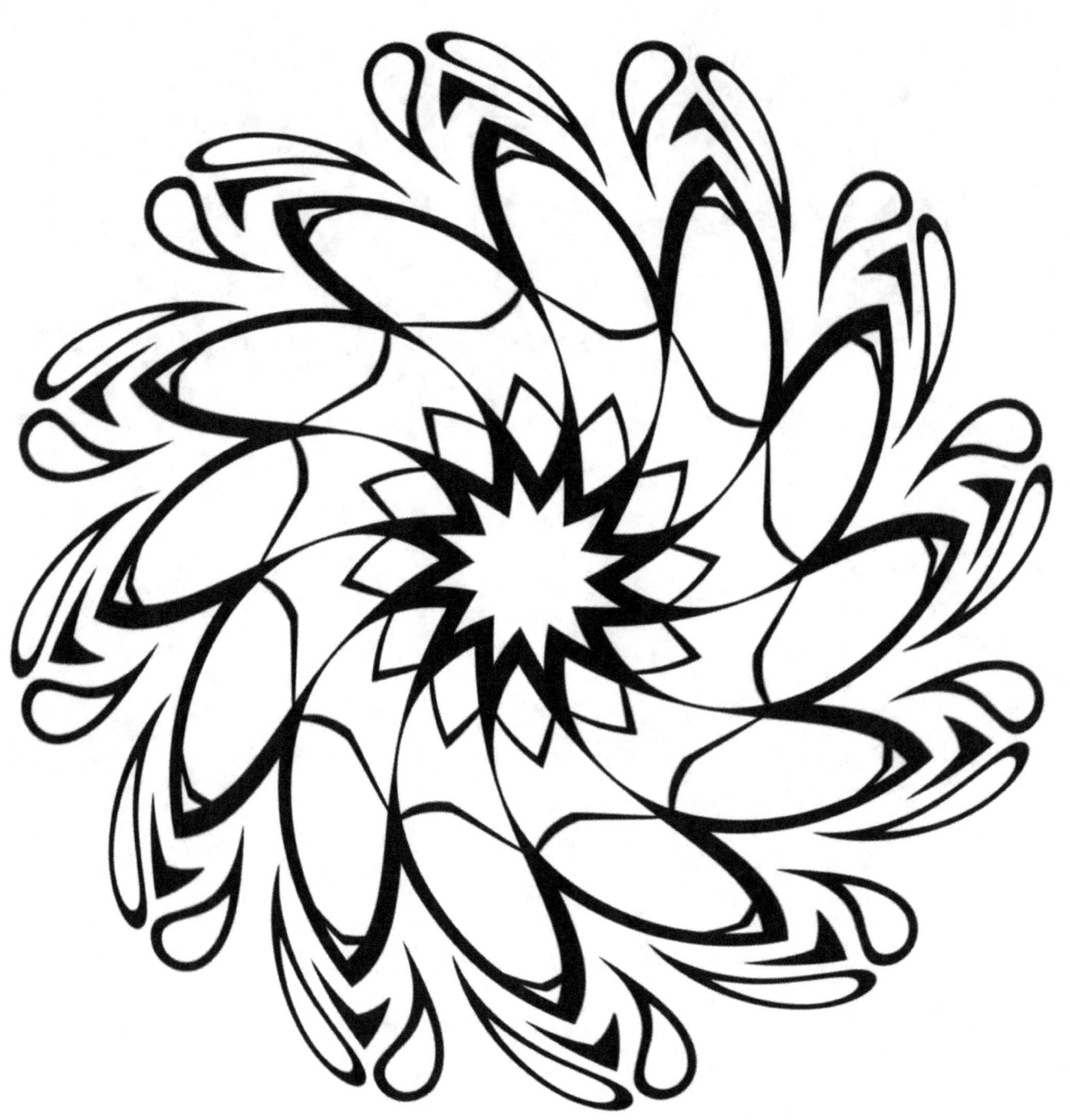

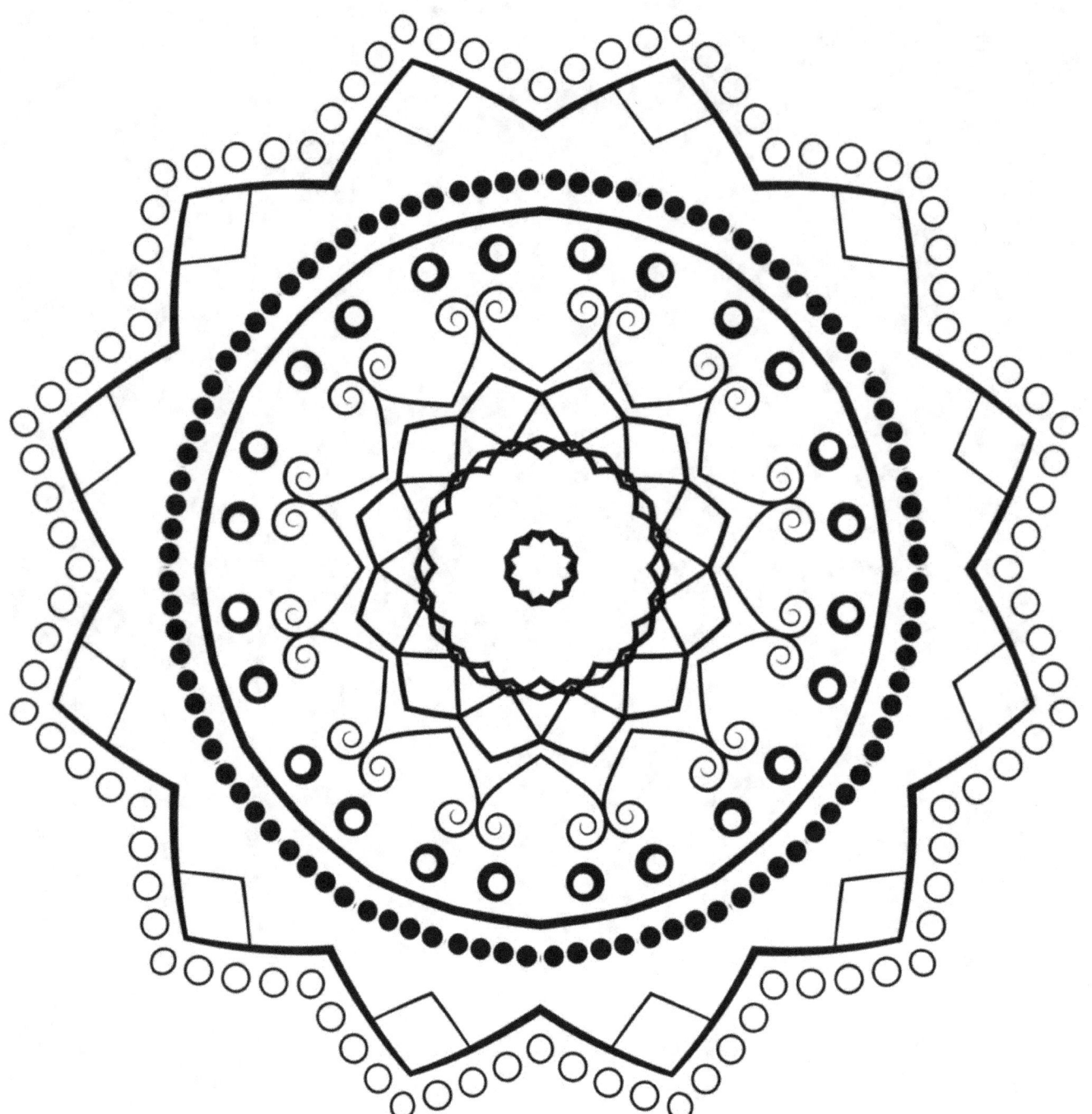

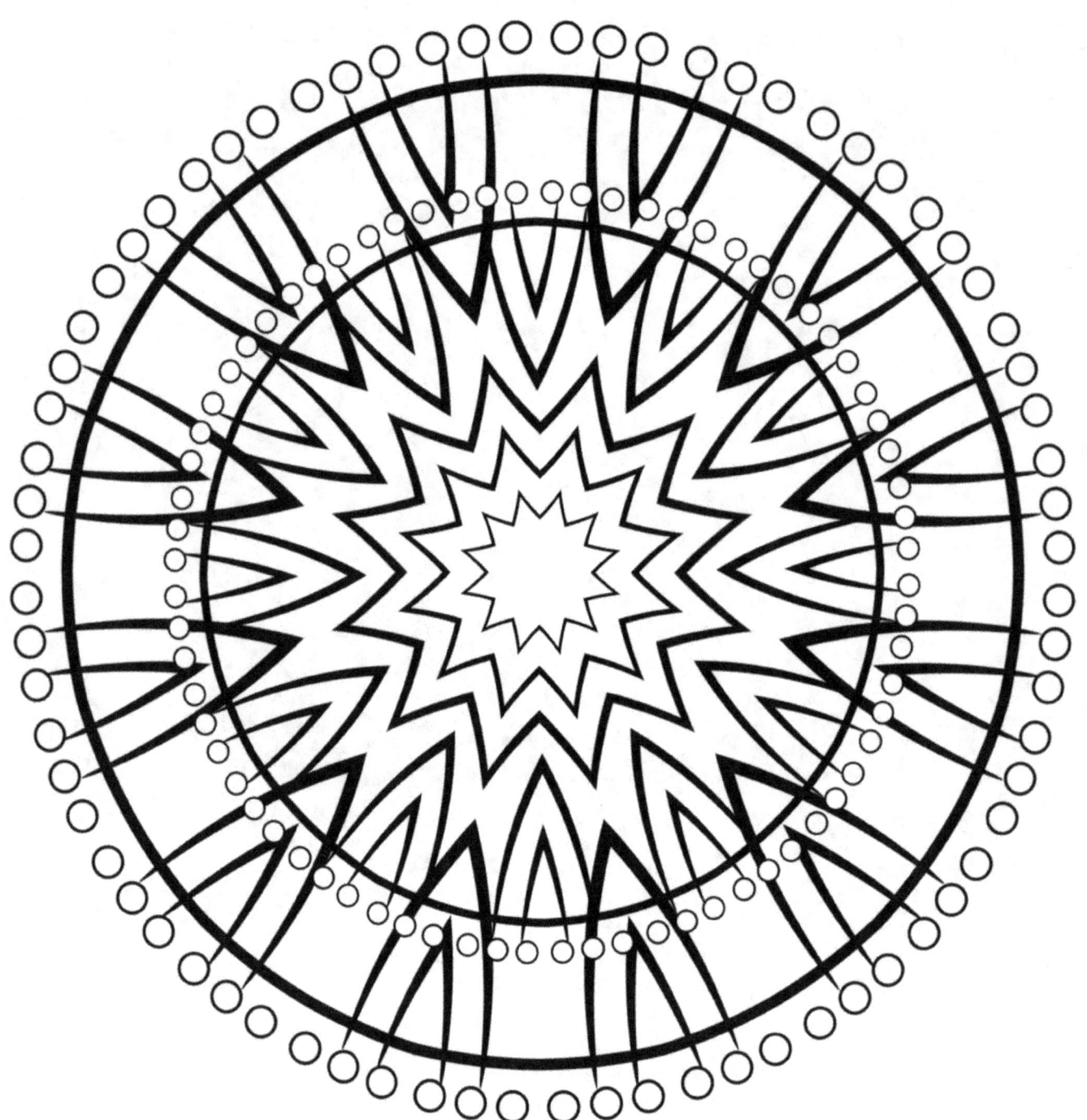

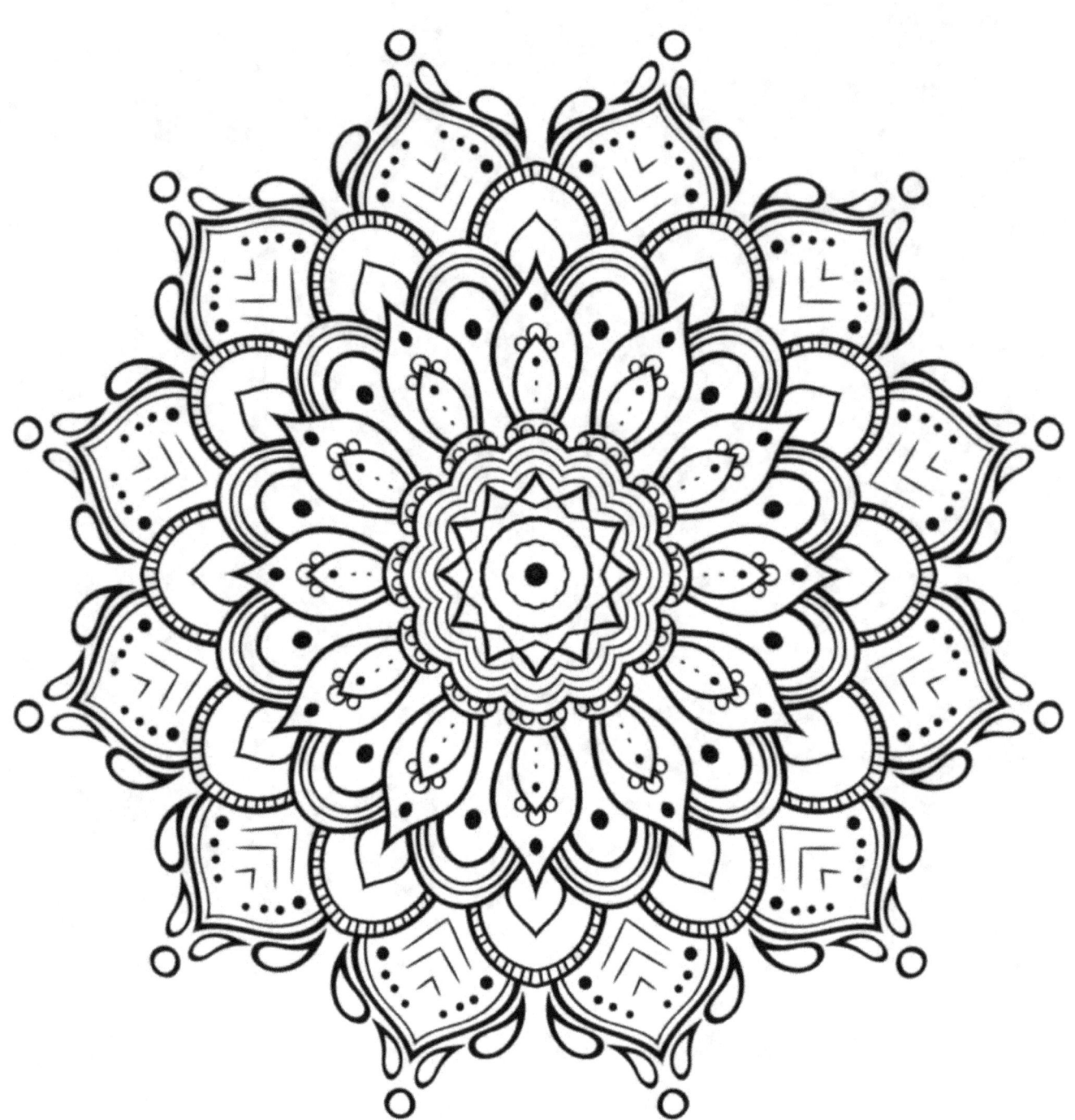

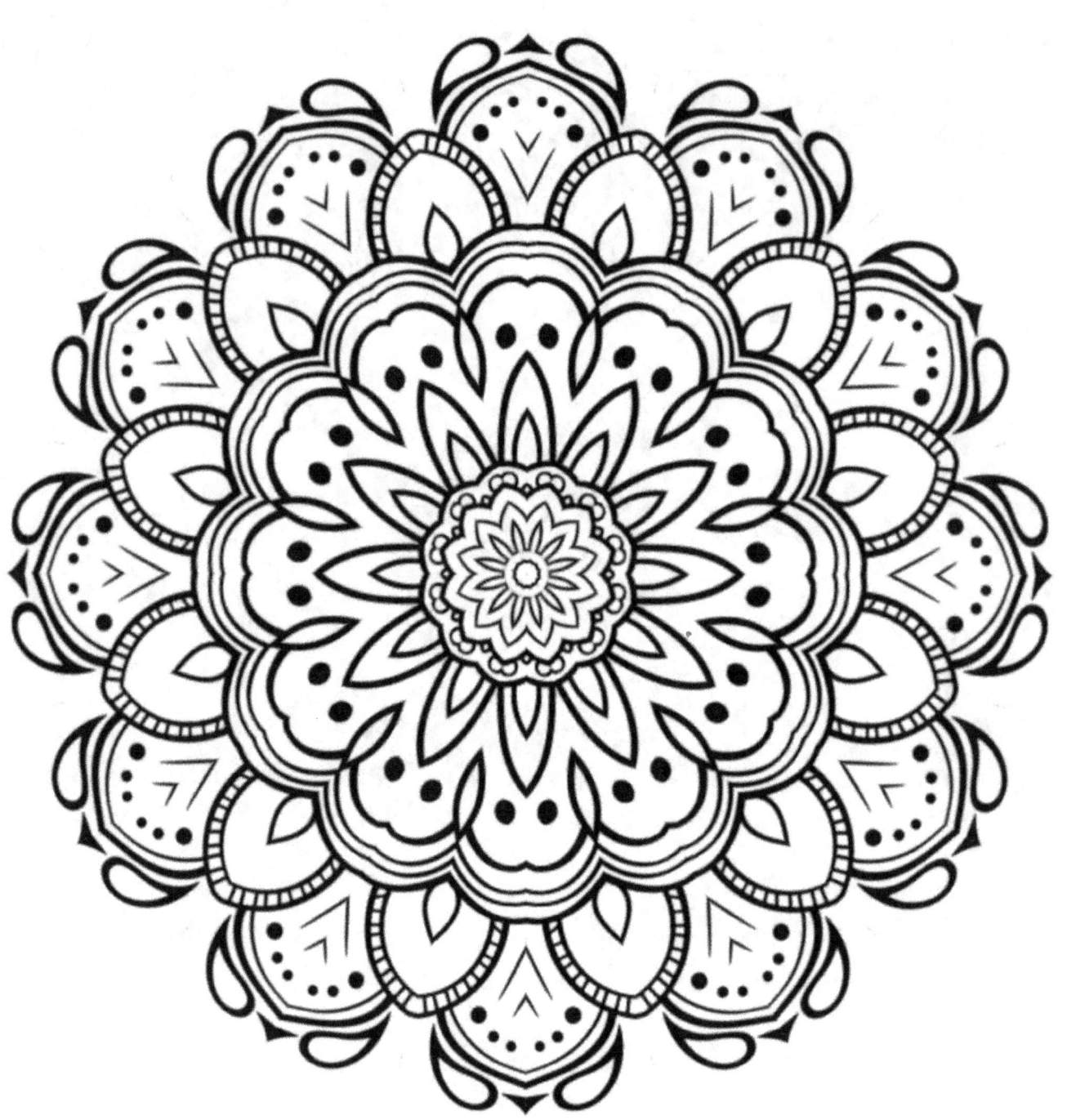

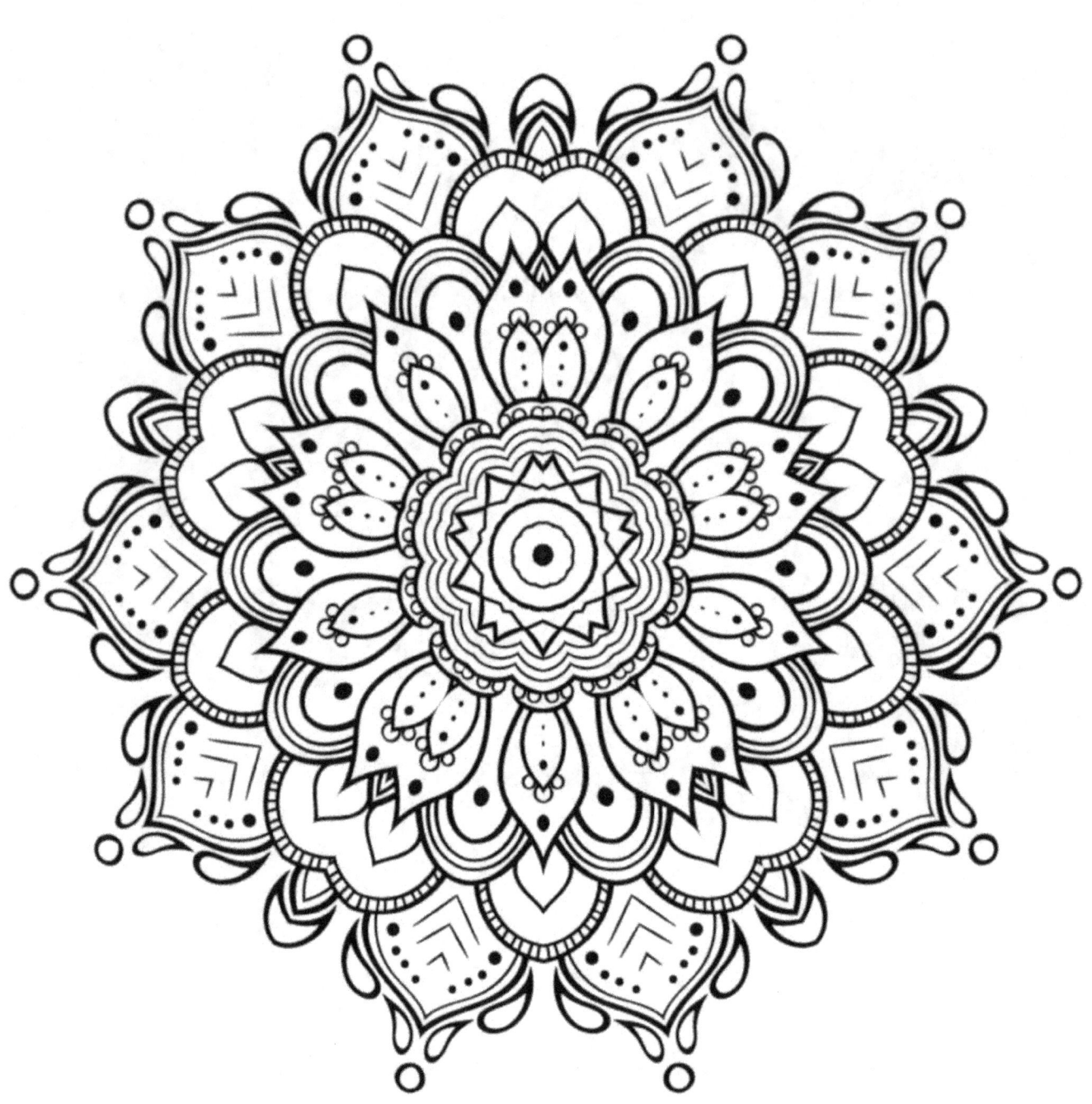

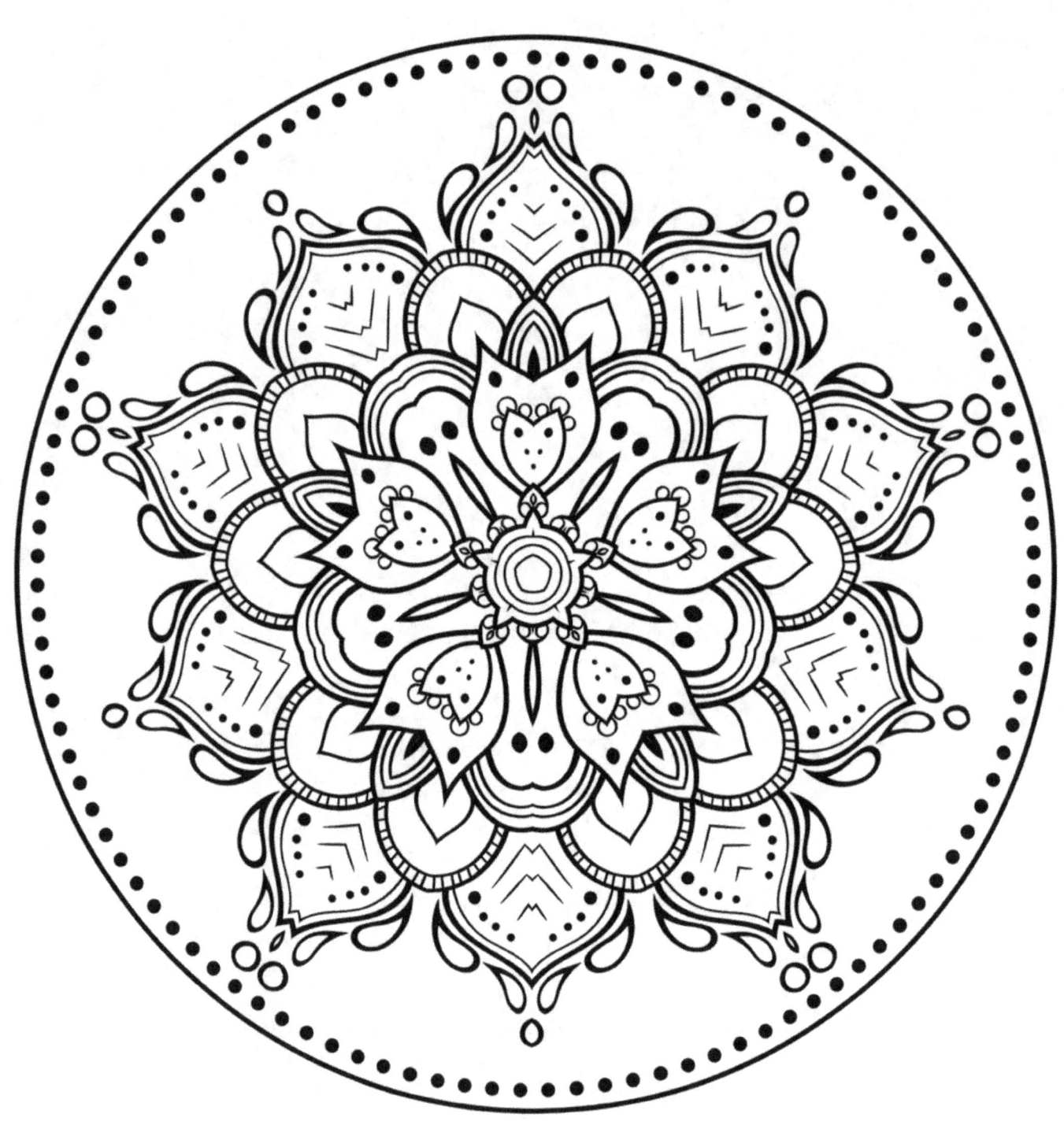

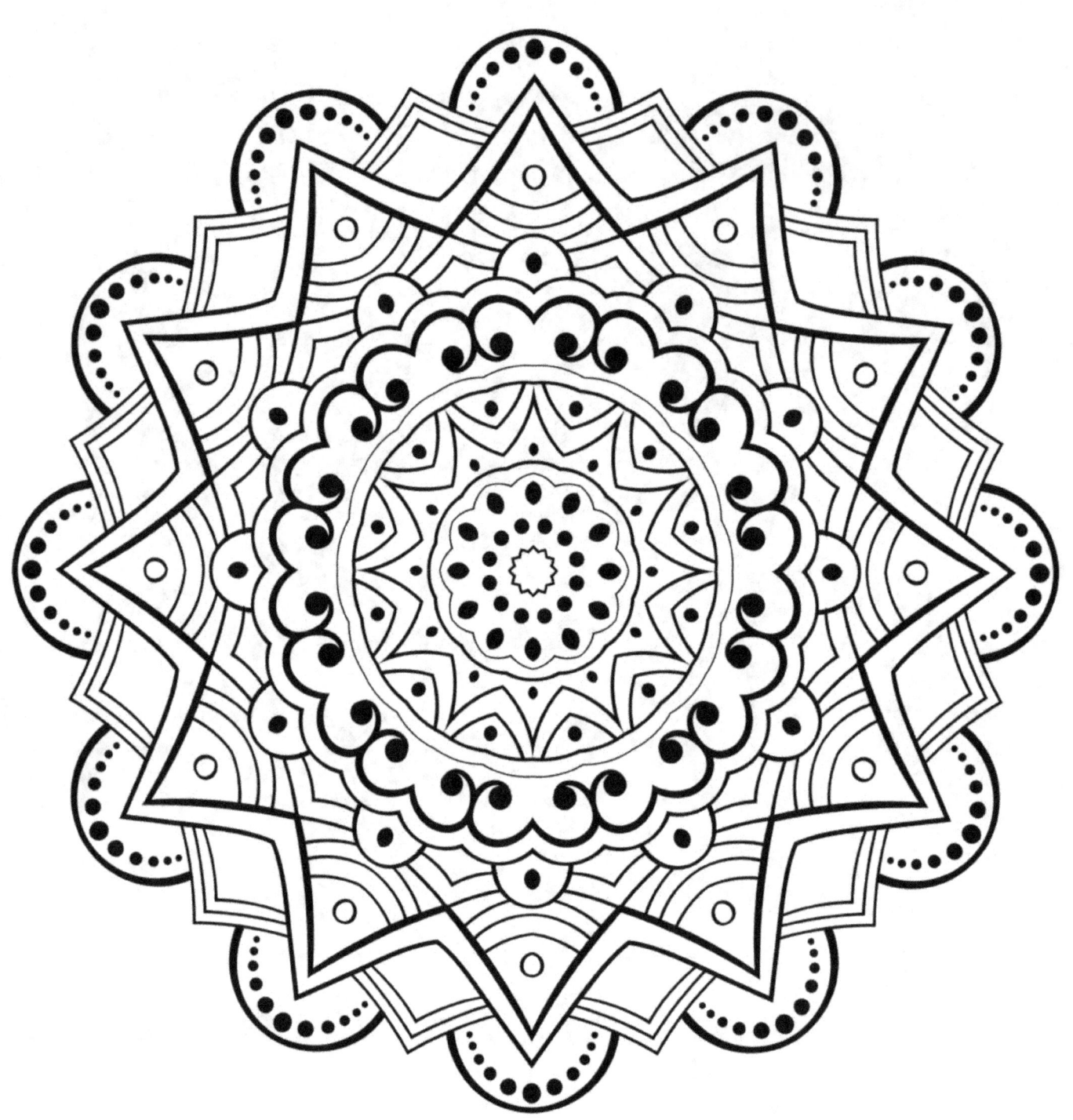

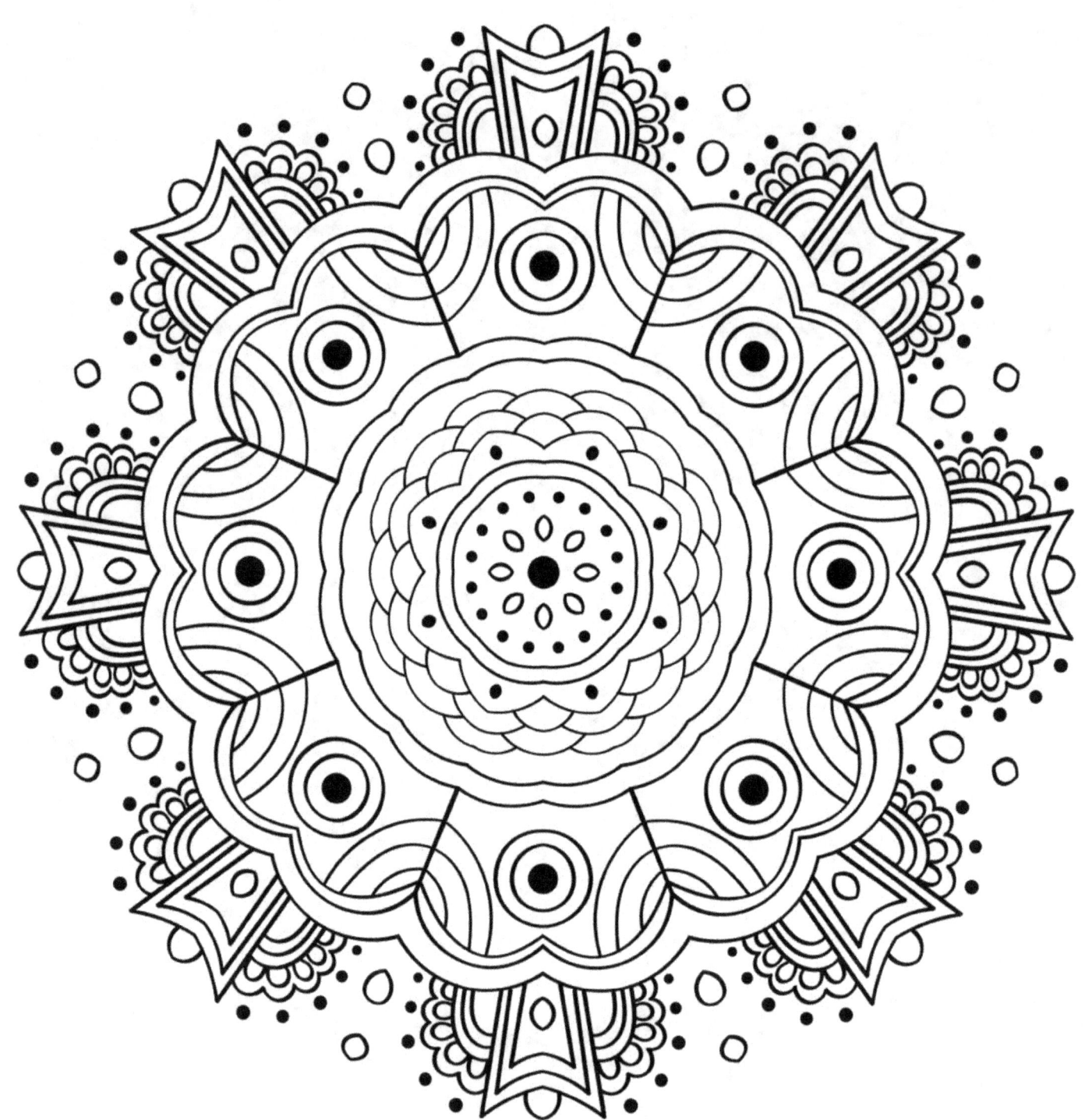

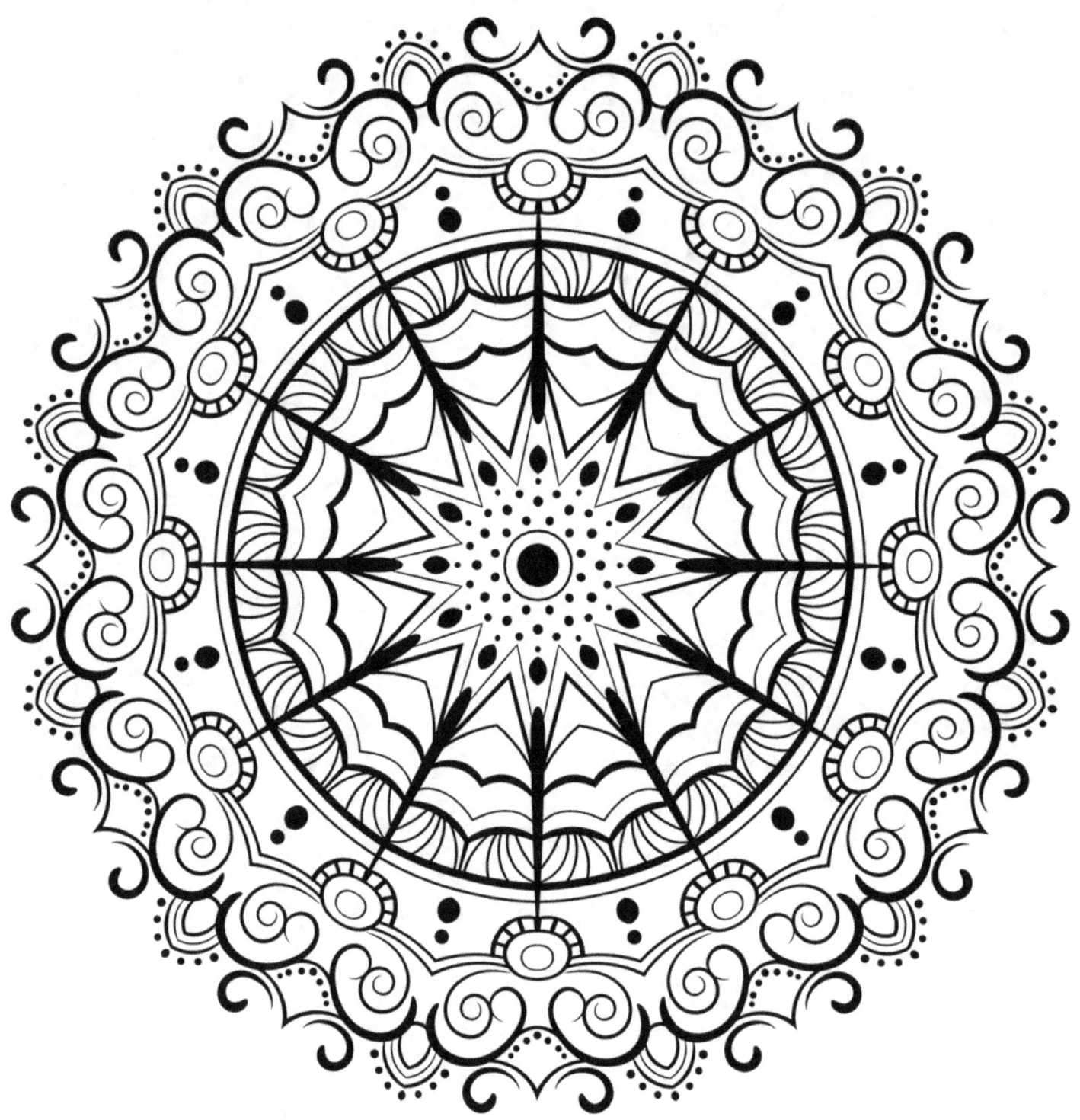

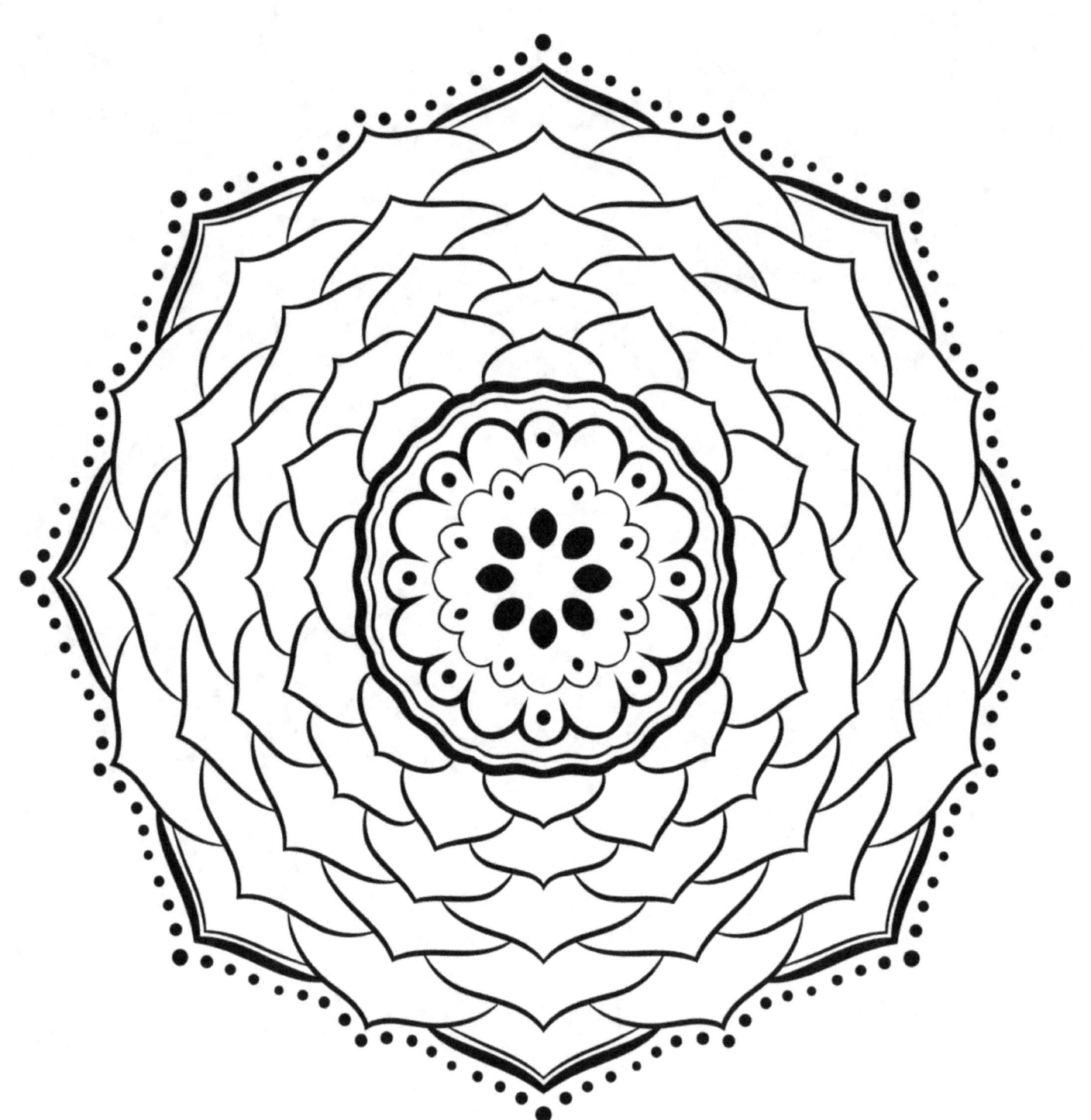

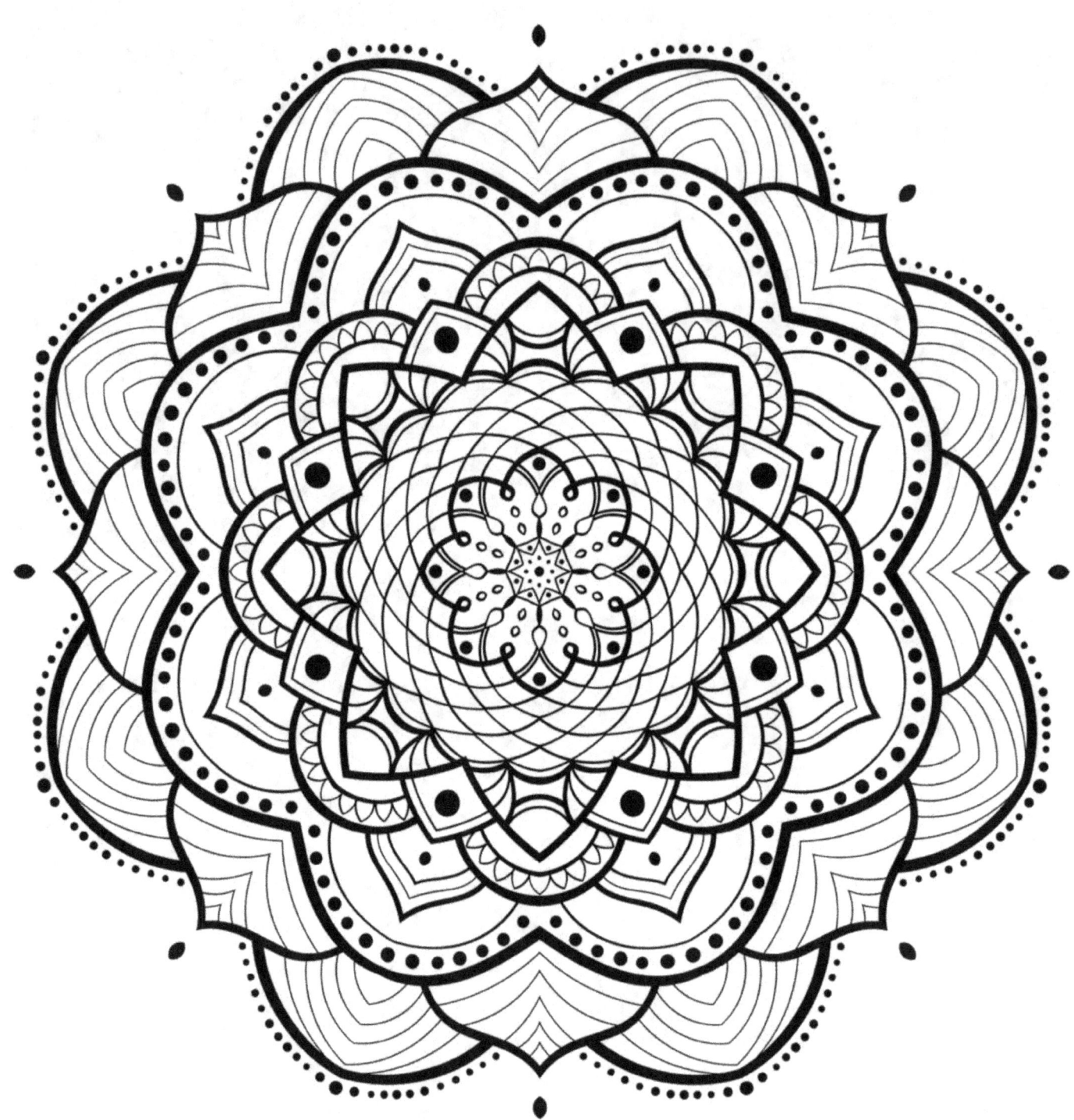

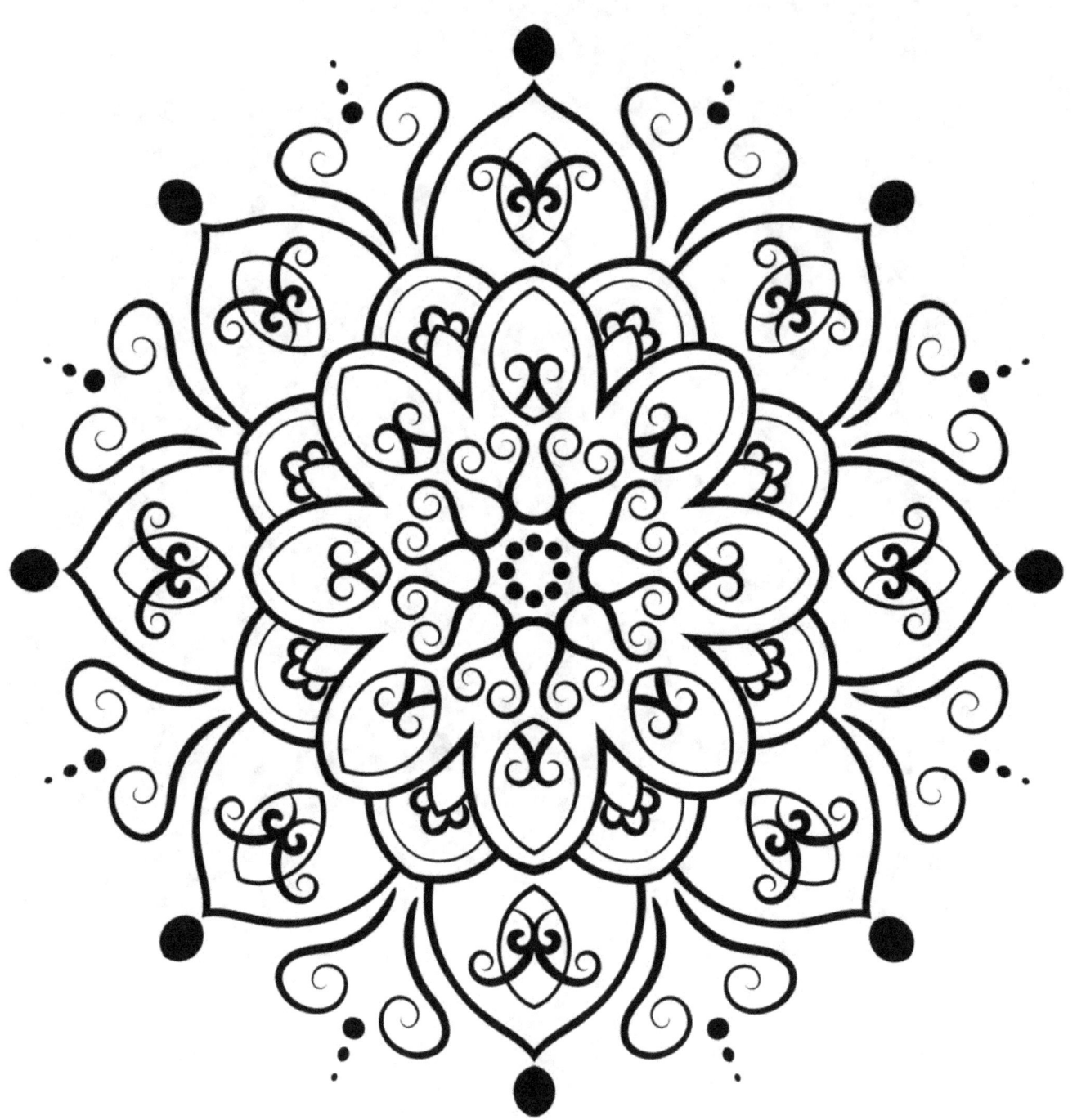

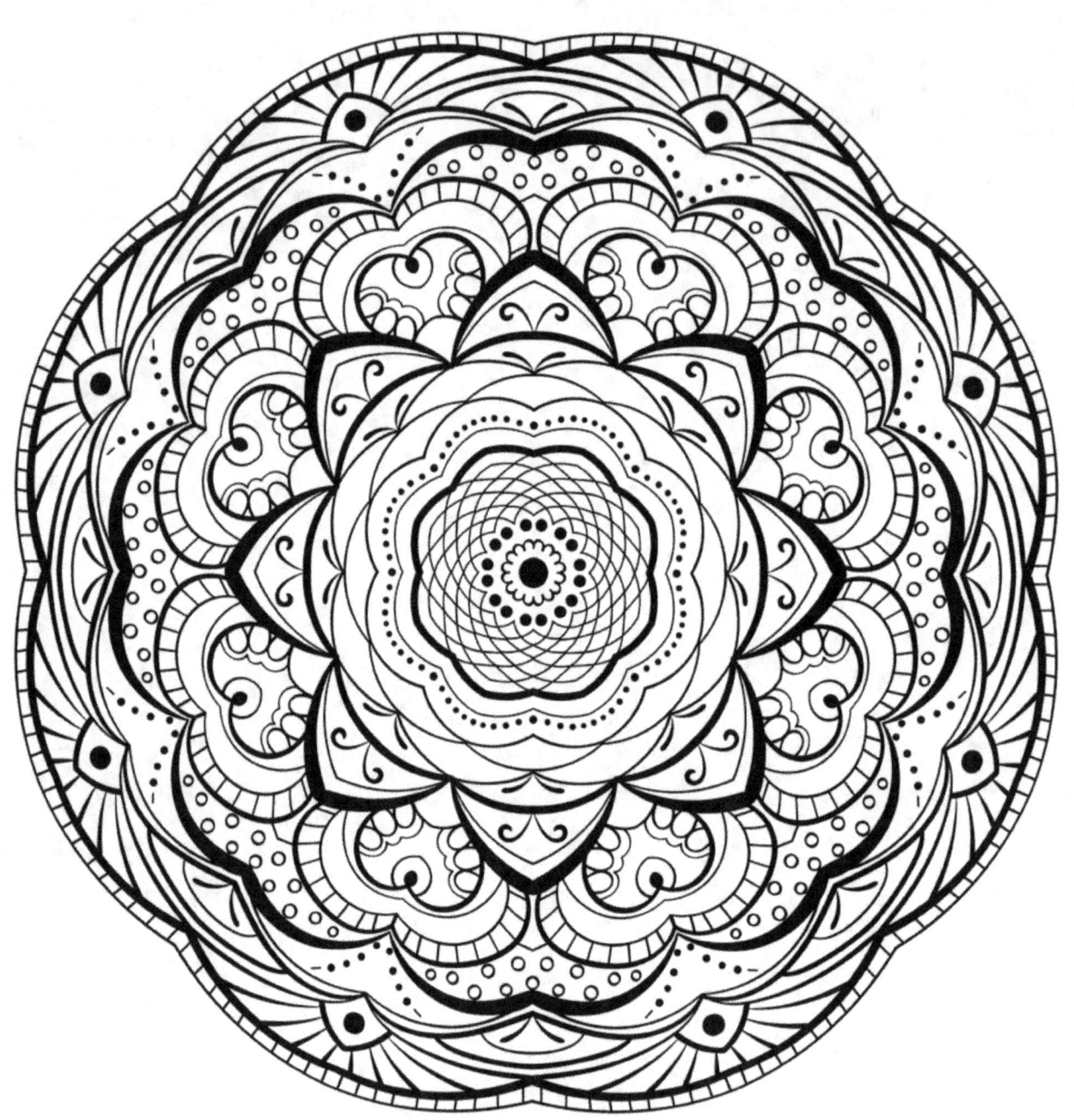

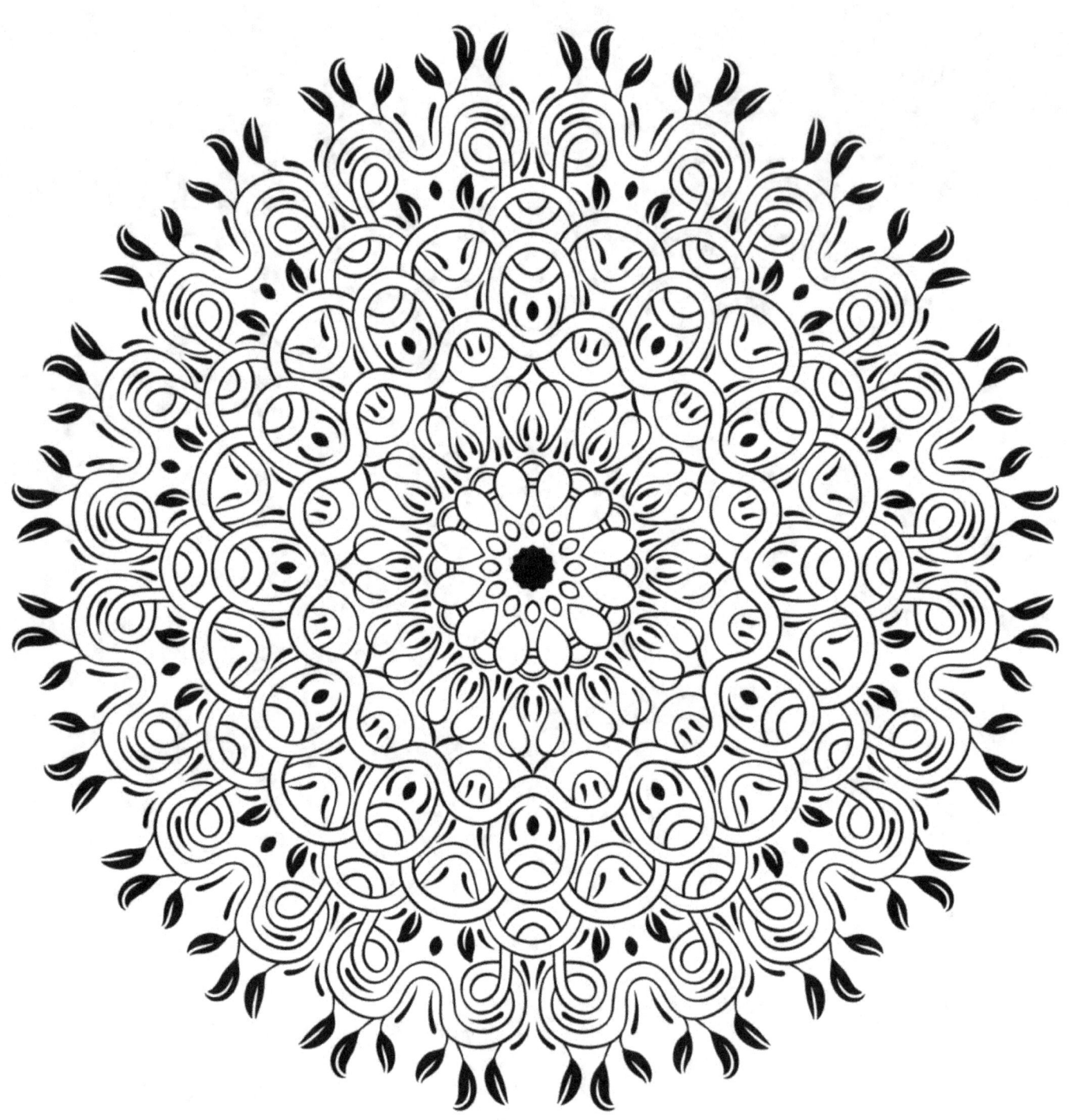

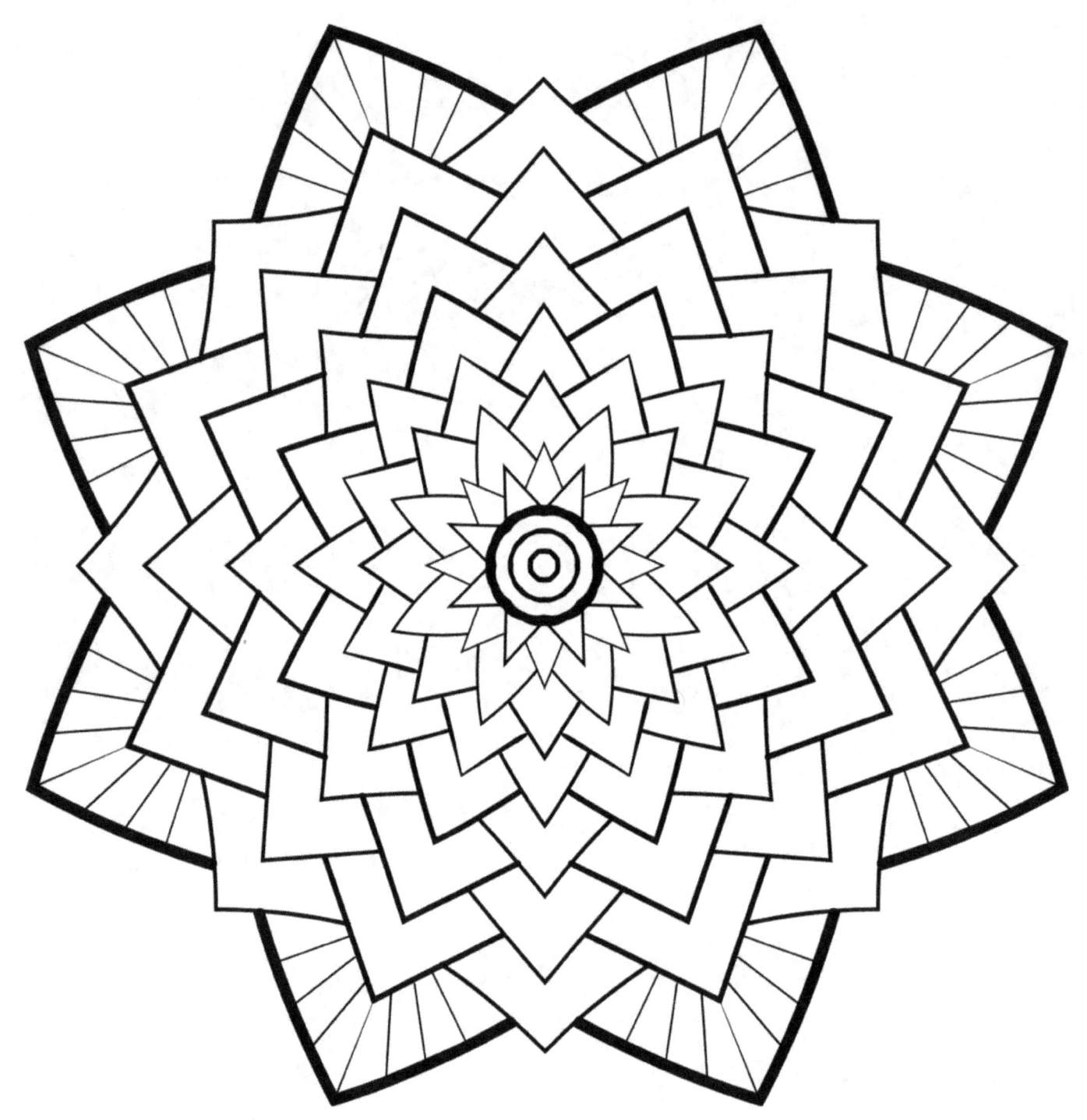